the home
kebob
cookbook

the home kebob cookbook

by beth merriman

Published in Association
with *Parade Magazine*

GALAHAD BOOKS • NEW YORK CITY

Contents

Foreword

It was years ago that I tasted my first kebob but I shall never forget it. On a beautiful, secluded beach near Old Saybrook, Connecticut, with a delicious salt breeze freshening the hot summer air, my friends built a miniature rock fireplace and started a driftwood fire. Soon the smell of bacon, onion and sizzling beef plus the fragrance of coffee raised our appetites to heights unknown before. Nothing had ever tasted so good before—perhaps it never will again!

Cooking meat on a stick undoubtedly originated with primitive man, soon after he learned how to build and light a fire. He may have dropped a chunk of raw meat into the fire, fished it out and liked the taste so much that he began spearing chunks with green sticks and holding the meat over the fire. We'll never know for sure, anymore than we can prove the Chinese version of the origin of roast pig, but it seems a logical idea.

In any event, the custom of grilling meat (and vegetables—even fruits) spread throughout the world. Known by various names, you will find it in Russia as *shashlik*, often grilled on a sword and flamed before serving. In the Near East the term is *shish kebab*, shish meaning skewer, and kebab, specially prepared meat. It is said that in this part of the world the method was originated by hungry soldiers gathered around fires on the battlefield. In Japan the word *yakimono* means broiled food and this food is often impaled on skewers. The French use the term *en brochette* for skewered food while in Indonesia and other parts of southeast Asia the term is *saté*. In Hungary *rablo-hus* and in Serbia, *razinjici* and *ceoapcici* (if you can pronounce them!) mean skewered foods. The Turks say *kebap*, the South Africans *sasaties*. In England the savories following dessert are sometimes skewered foods. The Greeks have a word for tidbits cooked on a skewer—*souvlakia*.

But in this country the kebob is king! It has grown in popularity by leaps and bounds until today it is the prime favorite of all alfresco foods. And no wonder, because the necessary equipment is inexpensive and the kebobs are easy to make. Much of the work can be done before it is time to cook them—and everybody likes them!

It is my fond hope that you will enjoy the recipes in this book, and that kebob dinners, indoors and out, will become favorites in your family.

BETH MERRIMAN

Equipment Needed For Making Kebobs

Brushes of different sizes are needed for basting kebobs as they grill. A small paint brush of good quality is recommended, but be sure the bristles are not plastic.

Bunches of fresh herbs tied to a long stick add aromatic flavor when used for basting.

Skewers are available in many sizes. In an emergency, long, peeled, green sticks with pointed tips may be used. The best skewers are made of steel and come in different lengths; some are handsome implements with decorative handles. Two-tined skewers help to hold food securely. Bamboo or wooden skewers should be thoroughly soaked before using, and one end of each should be sharpened.

Skewer racks are available. These are placed on the grid to support the skewers and make them easier to turn. Long handled, hinged grills adapt to kebobs of various thickness and make turning easy.

How To Build
A Charcoal Fire

Cover the bottom of the grill or fireplace with gravel to a depth of about ¾ inch. After about six uses, wash the gravel in hot water; spread out to dry.

Start making the fire at least 45 minutes before you intend to begin cooking. Build a pyramid of good quality briquets about 12 inches in diameter at the bottom and 6 inches high. Use a safe liquid fire starter on the briquets (never use alcohol, kerosene or gasoline) and ignite. When the flame has died down, let the briquets burn for about ½ hour. Then spread out the briquets in a single layer over the gravel. Soon they will be covered with a fine, gray ash. Before starting to cook, tap the briquets to remove this gray ash. Keep additional briquets warming at the edge of the fire. Add them about 15 minutes before you need them.

Never add liquid fuels to the briquets after the fire has been ignited. Never burn charcoal inside the house, even in an hibachi, unless the hibachi is set in a fireplace where a draft will pull all fumes up the chimney.

Helpful Hints

Start your fire at least 45 minutes before you begin to cook.

Grease skewers either by running them through a piece of suet or oiling them lightly, so that the cooked food will slide off easily.

Cut onions from the stem down to keep them from falling apart.

Parboil certain vegetables such as small whole onions, potatoes, sweet potatoes, zucchini, etc., before broiling or grilling.

Kebobs need a hot fire, so be sure coals are glowing under the coating of ash.

Balance the foods by weight on the skewer as you thread them.

Remember to rotate the skewers often and brush the kebob each time with a sauce or marinade.

Recipes
For Kebobs

ACCOMPANIMENTS

Fruit Kebobs

Select any combination of the following fruits and thread onto small skewers. Brush with melted butter or margarine and broil, or grill 4 inches above coals just long enough to heat through and lightly brown: banana chunks, small firm apricot halves, orange sections, grapefruit sections, apple chunks, pineapple chunks, chunks of fresh peaches or halves of pitted plums. All are good accompaniments to pork or ham.

Vegetable Kebobs

Select any combination of the following vegetables and thread onto skewers. Brush with melted butter or margarine and broil or grill until vegetables are soft and golden brown, turning and basting often: small canned white potatoes, chunks of parboiled sweet potatoes, small canned white onions, mushroom crowns, zucchini slices, cherry tomatoes, eggplant chunks, 1-inch slices of celery. If desired, 1-inch squares of bacon may be skewered between pieces of vegetables. If you wish, a marinade of bottled Italian dressing (in which vegetables have been soaked 1 hour before cooking) may be used in place of butter or margarine.

Variation: Parboil sweet potatoes; cool; peel; cut into cubes; alternate on skewers with fresh or canned pineapple cubes. Brush with melted butter or margarine; grill.

APPETIZERS

1. Cooked shrimp, 1-inch slices cooked rock lobster tails, raw scallops, half-strips of bacon. Wrap each piece of seafood with bacon and thread 3 or 4 onto short skewers. Grill 4 or 5 inches above coals until bacon is crisp and brown.

2. Halved, sautéed chicken livers, chunks of cooked chicken, water chestnuts and pineapple chunks. Wrap in half slices of bacon, skewer and grill as above.

3. Vienna sausages, watermelon pickles, artichoke hearts, canned mushroom crowns. Proceed as in 1, above.

4. Cooked turkey cubes, stuffed olives, Vienna sausages, canned mushroom crowns. Proceed as in 1, above.

Appetizer Kebobs

½ cup chicken broth
½ cup vinegar
¼ cup sugar
1 small onion, sliced
Salt to taste
2 teaspoons mixed pickling spices

24 carrot slices, ½ inch thick
2 cans (5 oz. each) water chestnuts, drained
24 slices bacon
12 chicken livers, halved
24 (1 inch) squares green pepper

Combine first 6 ingredients; bring to boil; simmer 15 minutes; strain; pour over carrots; simmer 10 minutes or until carrots are tender. Add water chestnuts; chill. Cook bacon; drain on absorbent paper. Measure ¼ cup bacon drippings; sauté chicken livers in drippings 5 minutes. Wrap each in a bacon slice. Thread a square of green pepper, a wrapped chicken liver, one water chestnut and one carrot slice onto each of 24 small skewers. *Serve at once.*

Japanese Appetizer Kebobs

Alternate 4 bite-size pieces of chicken and giblets on each bamboo skewer. (Wet the skewers thoroughly before using.) Grill on an hibachi, turning and brushing often with Sake Sauce*, until thoroughly cooked and brown. If available, sprinkle with powdered Japanese pepper.

*Sake Sauce

¼ cup sake (Japanese rice wine)	2½ tablespoons sugar
¼ cup soy sauce	

Combine all ingredients in small saucepan; stir over low heat until sugar dissolves. Boil for 1 minute.

Ham Teriyaki Appetizer Kebobs

2 pounds ham steak, cut into ¾-inch cubes	1 tablespoon grated onion
Salt and pepper	1 clove garlic, minced
1 cup grape jelly	2 teaspoons dry mustard
½ cup lemon juice	3 drops Tabasco

Spear 3 meat cubes on each small bamboo skewer. Sprinkle meat with salt and pepper. Place kebobs in a single layer in a shallow pan. Combine remaining ingredients; heat until jelly melts and sauce is smooth. Pour hot sauce over skewered meat. Let stand at room temperature for 1 hour. Turn meat several times to coat evenly. Drain meat; broil for 3 to 5 minutes on each side. *Serve immediately. Makes 16 appetizers.*

Yugoslav Kebobs

½ **cup finely chopped onions**	1 **pound lean beef, ground**
½ **teaspoon minced garlic**	1 **egg white, lightly beaten**
2 **tablespoons vegetable oil**	1 **teaspoon salt**
	1 **tablespoon paprika**
1 **pound lamb, ground**	2 **tablespoons minced onion**

Cook ½ cup chopped onions and garlic in oil until onions are a light yellow color; transfer to large bowl. Add lamb, beef, egg white, salt and paprika to pan in which onions were cooked. Mix well; cool enough to handle; shape into small "sausages" about 2 inches long and 1 inch in diameter. Chill until firm. Thread onto skewers, running the skewers through sides, not ends, of the cylinders and leaving a space of ¼ inch between "sausages." Grill 4 inches above coals, turning once, for about 8 minutes on each side. Slide off skewers onto plates. Sprinkle with minced onion. *Serve as hot hors d'oeuvres.*

BEEF

Beef Kebobs

1 can (20 oz.) pineapple chunks	18 mushroom caps
3 pounds tender beef, cut into 1½-inch cubes	18 cherry tomatoes
	2 large green peppers, cut into 1½-inch squares

Drain pineapple and reserve juice. Add enough water to juice to make 1 cup and add to Marinade* ingredients. Pour over meat; cover and refrigerate for 2 to 4 hours. Alternate meat, vegetables and pineapple on skewers. Place each kebob on sheet of heavy-duty aluminum foil. Spoon remaining marinade over kebobs. Bring up foil, double-fold top and ends to seal. Place on grill about 3 inches above coals. Grill for 30 minutes, turning frequently. *Makes 6 servings. Serve with:* shoestring potatoes, corn on the cob and coleslaw.

*Marinade

⅓ cup cider vinegar	3 tablespoons soy sauce
½ cup catchup	¼ teaspoon Tabasco
⅓ cup brown sugar	Heavy-duty aluminum foil
Juice of 1 lemon	

Combine all ingredients; mix well.

Barbecued Beef Kebobs

2 pounds packaged
stew meat *or* top or
bottom round, cut
1½ inches thick
1 package instant
meat marinade
⅔ cup cold water

8 small onions,
parboiled 5 minutes
1 green pepper,
parboiled and cut into
8 squares
8 small fresh mushrooms
4 cherry tomatoes

If meat was not purchased already cubed, cut into ¾-to 1-inch cubes. Blend contents of package of instant meat marinade and water thoroughly in a shallow pan. Place meat cubes in marinade. Pierce all surfaces of meat thoroughly with fork to carry flavor deep-down and to lock in natural juices. Marinate for only 15 minutes, turning several times. Remove meat from marinade; drain. Reserve marinade for basting. Lace meat alternately with vegetables (except tomato) onto skewers. Allow 4 cubes of meat per skewer. Brush entire skewer with marinade or roll entire skewer in marinade. Place on barbecue grill 3 inches from hot coals. Barbecue for 8 to 12 minutes, turning and brushing frequently with marinade. During last 5 minutes of cooking, top each skewer with cherry tomato. *Makes 4 servings. Serve with:* potatoes julienne, coleslaw and hot garlic bread.

Teriyaki Variation

Combine contents of package of instant meat marinade with water; blend-in ½ teaspoon each dry mustard and ginger, 2 tablespoons molasses, 1 medium clove garlic, minced or pressed; mix well. Place kebobs in marinade and proceed as above. Complete the barbecue menu with baked beans, crispy French bread, salad greens and garlic croutons tossed with tart oil-vinegar dressing. For dessert—fresh fruit in season or peach shortcake with lots of hot coffee.

Beef 'N Bacon Kebobs

Spicy Tomato Sauce*
1 package (6 oz.)
   curried rice mix
1 pound lean
   ground beef
1 garlic clove, minced
½ teaspoon salt
¼ teaspoon pepper
½ pound sliced bacon
1 can (13½ oz.)
   pineapple chunks,
   drained
3 dill pickles, quartered

Prepare Spicy Tomato Sauce and keep hot; prepare rice according to package directions and keep hot. Combine beef, garlic, salt and pepper; shape into 16 meatballs. Onto 4 10-inch skewers, lace bacon with meatballs, pineapple and pickles, beginning and ending with meatballs. Brush kebobs with Spicy Tomato Sauce; arrange on broiler rack 5 inches from heat. Broil for about 15 minutes, turning and basting often with sauce. Meanwhile, toss rice with remaining pineapple chunks. Serve with kebobs. *Makes 4 servings.* *Add:* broccoli, celery and carrot sticks.

*Spicy Tomato Sauce

1 can (8 oz.)
   tomato sauce
2 tablespoons brown
   sugar
2 tablespoons vinegar
1 tablespoon Worcester-
   shire sauce
2 teaspoons instant
   minced onion
1 teaspoon chili powder

In small saucepan combine all ingredients. Heat to boiling; reduce heat, keeping hot while making kebobs.

Beef And Walnut Kebobs

2 pounds lean beef,
   ground
1 garlic clove, crushed
½ cup finely chopped
   onion
1 cup chopped walnuts
2 eggs
1 teaspoon salt
Dash Tabasco
Melted butter *or*
   margarine

Combine all ingredients except butter; mix well. Chill until firm. Shape into small balls or "sausages;" string onto skewers. Brush with melted butter. Broil or grill 4 inches from heat, turning often and brushing with melted butter, for about 10 to 12 minutes. *Serve with:* French fried potatoes, zucchini Creole and a green salad.

Beef And Lobster Kebobs
With Sauce Tyrol

1 **package (1 lb.) lean beef stew meat** *or*
1 **pound top** *or* **bottom round, cut into 1½-inch cubes**
Instant seasoned meat tenderizer
1 **package (10 to 12 oz.) frozen rock lobster tails, thawed**

4 **fresh mushrooms**
1 **cup catchup**
⅓ **cup vegetable oil**
2 **tablespoons wine vinegar**
½ **cup mayonnaise** *or* **salad dressing**

Moisten meat thoroughly with water. Sprinkle meat tenderizer evenly, like salt, on all sides. Use no salt. To insure penetration, pierce meat cubes deeply with kitchen fork. Remove lobster from shells; proceed as above with meat tenderizer; cut into 1½-inch chunks. Thread meat cubes and lobster chunks alternately on four 10- to 12-inch skewers, ending with a mushroom. Combine catchup and next 2 ingredients for sauce; reserve 2 tablespoons; brush one side of kebobs with sauce; place on grill set 3 inches above hot coals. Barbecue for 12 to 15 minutes, turning and basting frequently with sauce until lobster flakes easily with fork. Add the 2 tablespoons of reserved sauce to mayonnaise; serve with kebobs. *Makes 4 servings. Serve with:* hot garlic bread, mixed vegetables and endive stuffed with Old English cheese spread.

Marinated Beef And Pineapple Kebobs

1½ pounds tender, lean beef
2 cups tomato juice
½ cup wine vinegar
¼ cup prepared mustard
2 teaspoons salt
2 teaspoons sugar
¼ teaspoon Tabasco
½ pound fresh medium mushrooms
Pineapple chunks

Cut beef into 1-inch cubes. Combine all remaining ingredients except mushrooms and pineapple; pour over beef cubes. Cover; refrigerate for 2 hours. Drain beef, saving marinade. Alternate beef cubes and pineapple chunks on skewers; end with mushrooms. Grill 4 inches above coals for 12 to 15 minutes, turning often and basting with marinade. *Makes 4 servings. Serve with:* baked potatoes, sweet-sour cucumber and onion slices and hot garlic bread.

Burgundy Kebobs

2 pounds ground beef
1 cup rolled oats
2 teaspoons salt
¼ teaspoon seasoned pepper
2 tablespoons prepared mustard
2 tablespoons prepared horseradish
2 eggs
48 small stuffed olives
Burgundy Marinade *
32 canned broiled mushroom crowns

Combine first 7 ingredients. Shape around olives to make 48 small balls. Cover with marinade. Chill for several hours. Drain, saving marinade. Thread onto skewers, using 3 meatballs and 2 mushroom crowns on each. Grill 4 inches above heat to desired degree of doneness, turning once, carefully, and brushing with marinade several times. *Makes 8 servings. Serve with:* hot potato salad and coleslaw.

*Burgundy Marinade

1 tablespoon cornstarch
2 tablespoons cold water
3 tablespoons wine vinegar
1½ tablespoons light brown sugar

1 cup Burgundy
1 small onion, sliced thin
2 peppercorns, crushed
1 small bay leaf, crushed
¼ teaspoon oregano
¼ teaspoon salt

Blend cornstarch and cold water. Add vinegar, sugar and wine. Cook and stir over low heat until thickened and clear. Remove from heat. Add remaining ingredients; cool. Pour over meatballs. Chill.

Galley Kebobs

2 cans (15 oz. each) meatballs in gravy
1 can (8 oz.) tomato sauce with onions
1 teaspoon brown sugar *or* maple-blended syrup

1 teaspoon vinegar
1 can (4 oz.) whole mushrooms, drained
1 can (1 lb.) whole small carrots, drained and halved crosswise

Drain gravy from meatballs into 12-inch skillet; reserve meatballs. Stir in tomato sauce with onions, brown sugar and vinegar. On each of 6 skewers alternate 4 mushrooms, 3 meatballs and 2 carrot pieces. Add any remaining mushrooms and meatballs to skillet, crumbling meatballs into sauce. Arrange kebobs in skillet; simmer 15 to 20 minutes or until thoroughly heated, turning kebobs once or twice. *Makes 4 to 6 servings. Serve with:* instant mashed potatoes and green beans vinaigrette.

Cowboy Kebobs

3 pounds top round, cut 1 inch thick
Instant meat tenderizer
1½ cups claret
½ cup soy sauce
1 cup vegetable oil
1½ teaspoons powdered ginger
¼ teaspoon garlic powder
¼ cup instant minced onion
2 teaspoons salt
½ teaspoon coarse black pepper
24 small cooked or canned onions
4 green peppers, cut into 24 squares
8 cherry tomatoes
8 fresh medium mushroom caps

Remove excess fat from beef. Cut into cubes (you will need 32). Treat with tenderizer as directed on container. Combine next 8 ingredients; mix well; pour over beef cubes. Let stand for at least 2 hours. Drain, saving marinade. Alternate 4 beef cubes, 3 onions and 3 green pepper squares on each of 8 long skewers, beginning and ending with beef cubes. Broil over charcoal for about 15 minutes, turning often to brown on all sides, brushing frequently with marinade. During last 5 minutes put a cherry tomato and mushroom cap on end of each skewer. *Makes 8 servings. Serve with:* Lyonnaise potatoes, corn on the cob and a salad of crisp greens.

Rodeo Beef Kebobs

4 to 5 pounds chuck roast, boned and cut into 1½-inch cubes (16 cubes)
Seasoned instant meat tenderizer
3 tablespoons vegetable oil
3 tablespoons dry sherry
2 tablespoons Worcestershire sauce
½ teaspoon oregano

Prepare all surfaces of the meat, one side at a time, as follows: Thoroughly moisten meat with water. Sprinkle instant meat tenderizer evenly, like salt, over the entire surface of the meat. Use no salt. To insure penetration and to retain meat juices, pierce meat deeply and thoroughly with a kitchen fork at about ½-inch intervals. Meat is ready for cooking immediately. Lace meat cubes onto 4 10-to 12-inch metal skewers. Allow at least 4 cubes of meat per skewer. Combine remaining ingredients for basting sauce. Brush skewered meat with basting sauce and place on grill set 1 to 2 inches above coals. Barbecue for 8 to 12 minutes, turning and basting frequently with sauce. *Makes 4 servings. Serve with:* foil-baked potatoes, tossed salad, drizzled with French dressing and baked apples cooked over the coals in foil.

Peppy Beef Kebobs

2 **pounds lean beef
  (round *or* chuck)**
**Instant unseasoned
  meat tenderizer**
½ **cup vegetable oil**
¼ **cup wine vinegar**
¼ **cup minced onion**
1 **teaspoon salt**
Dash Tabasco
2 **teaspoons thick
  steak sauce**

Cut beef into 1- to 1½-inch cubes. Treat with tenderizer according to directions. Combine remaining ingredients; pour over beef; let stand for at least 2 hours, turning often. Drain beef, saving marinade. String beef onto skewers. Grill 4 to 5 inches above hot coals for about 20 minutes, turning often and basting with marinade. Slide off skewers into toasted frankfurter rolls. *Makes 6 servings. Serve with:* potato salad and green pepper coleslaw.

Hamburger Kebobs

Form your favorite, firm meat loaf mixture into small balls, about 1½ inches in diameter. Thread the end of a slice of bacon onto skewers. String skewer with 4 meatballs and 4 pieces of onion. Weave bacon strip in and out around skewer and run skewer through the other end. Brush with Hamburger Sauce*. Grill until bacon is crisp, turning often and basting with sauce. Slide off skewers into toasted frankfurter rolls. *Serve with:* macaroni salad and raw vegetable relishes.

*Hamburger Sauce

2 tablespoons butter *or* margarine, melted	Dash Tabasco
	1 teaspoon onion powder
⅓ cup vegetable oil	1 tablespoon lemon juice
½ cup catchup	
1 tablespoon prepared mustard	1 teaspoon sugar

Combine all ingredients; mix well. *Makes about 1 cup.*

September Kebobs

¾ cup vegetable oil	1 garlic clove, crushed
6 tablespoons soy sauce	3 tablespoons lemon juice
2 tablespoons Worcestershire sauce	1 teaspoon sugar
	1 teaspoon savory
1 tablespoon dry mustard	Lean beef, cut into 1½-inch cubes
1 teaspoon salt	Half-strips of bacon
1 teaspoon coarsely ground black pepper	Thick slices of small tomatoes
	Squares of green and sweet red peppers
¼ cup wine vinegar	Medium mushroom crowns
¾ teaspoon dried parsley flakes	

Combine first 12 ingredients. Pour over beef cubes. Refrigerate for several hours or overnight. Drain, saving marinade. Wrap each beef cube in half-strip of bacon. Thread beef cubes and vegetables alternately onto long skewers. Brush with marinade. Grill 4 inches above hot coals for 15 to 20 minutes, turning often and brushing with marinade. The marinade will measure about 1¾ cups and can be doubled if desired. *Serve with:* potatoes baked in foil over coals, pickled beets and a stuffed celery salad.

Kebobs California

1½ **pounds beef chuck, cut into 1½-inch cubes**	1 **bay leaf**
Unseasoned meat tenderizer	1 **tablespoon minced onion**
1 **teaspoon dry mustard**	½ **cup vegetable oil**
½ **teaspoon salt**	1 **cup beer**
½ **teaspoon peppercorns**	1 **green pepper, cut into 1-inch squares**
¼ **teaspoon oregano**	3 **tomatoes, quartered**
	12 **small whole onions, parboiled**
	12 **whole mushrooms**

Treat beef with meat tenderizer according to label directions. Combine dry mustard, salt, peppercorns, oregano, bay leaf, onion, oil and beer; pour over beef. Marinate in refrigerator for 5 hours, or overnight. Drain, saving marinade. Alternate beef and vegetables on skewers. Place on grill about 4 inches above coals. Grill 10 minutes on each side, using marinade for basting. *Makes 6 servings. Serve with:* succotash and apple-raisin coleslaw.

Maxi California Beef Kebobs

2 pounds lean,
  boneless beef chuck
Unseasoned instant
  meat tenderizer
California Beef
  Basting Sauce*

Zucchini, green pepper,
  cherry tomatoes
French dressing

Remove excess fat from beef. Cut beef into 1½- to 2-inch cubes. Sprinkle with meat tenderizer, following label directions. Prick deeply with fork. Let stand at room temperature for about ½ hour. Thread beef onto skewers. Broil to desired degree of doneness. Brush often with California Beef Basting Sauce after beef begins to brown. Turn to brown all sides. Cut zucchini lengthwise, then crosswise. Cut green pepper into chunks, and leave tomatoes whole. Thread vegetables onto skewers and broil to desired degree of doneness. Baste with French dressing. *Makes 4 servings.*

*California Beef Basting Sauce

¼ cup vinegar
1 tablespoon
  Worcestershire sauce
2 tablespoons catchup
2 tablespoons dry
  sherry

1 tablespoon brown
  sugar
1 teaspoon prepared
  mustard
¼ cup maple-flavored
  syrup

Combine all ingredients, stirring to blend well. Heat and stir until sauce simmers. *Makes about ¾ cup.*

Skewered Beef In Marinade

2 pounds tender,
  lean beef
¼ cup grated onion
1 tablespoon
  crumbled dried basil

½ teaspoon salt
Dash Tabasco
⅓ cup red wine vinegar
⅔ cup vegetable oil

Cut beef into 1½-inch cubes. Combine remaining ingredients; mix well; pour over beef. Marinate for at least 5 hours, turning the beef often. Drain beef, saving marinade. Thread beef onto skewers; brush with marinade; grill 4 inches above coals for 10 to 15 minutes, turning often and brushing with marinade. *Makes 6 servings. Serve with:* kasha (buckwheat groats), orange and onion salad, grilled tomatoes.

Skewered Beef Round Alfresco

2 pounds beef top round, about 2 inches thick	¼ cup tarragon wine vinegar
	¼ cup sherry
	1 mashed garlic clove

Cut beef round into 2-inch squares. Combine vinegar, sherry and garlic. Pour over beef chunks, tossing to coat all sides. Let stand for 15 minutes. Thread onto skewers, leaving about an inch between beef squares. Grill on barbecue or in broiler, turning to brown all sides. Remove from skewer and cut into thin slices across the grain. *Makes about 4 servings. Serve with:* French bread and Chili Salsa*.

*Chili Salsa

¼ cup chopped green onion	1 cup drained chopped tomato
½ cup chopped green pepper	½ teaspoon salt
1 cup chopped celery	1 can (7 oz.) green chili salsa

Combine all ingredients. Chill for several hours. *Makes about 3 cups.*

Saybrook Shishkebob

Cut tenderized lean round steak into 1-inch cubes. Cut bacon strips crosswise into 1-inch pieces. Cut celery stalks crosswise into ½-inch pieces. Dice onion into ½-inch pieces. Use 8-inch skewers. Skewer steak, bacon, celery and onion and repeat until skewer is filled, beginning and ending with steak. Grill 3 inches above coals, turning often to cook on all sides; slip off skewers into toasted frankfurter rolls. *Serve with:* potato salad, deviled eggs and raw vegetable relishes.

Skillet Kebobs

1½ pounds top round
or top sirloin, cut
into 1½-inch cubes
1 large green
pepper, seeded and
cut into 8 pieces
12 fresh medium
mushroom caps
(3 per skewer)
4 cherry tomatoes
Brown 'n Season
3 tablespoons
vegetable oil
2 tablespoons prepared
mustard

Lace four 6-inch skewers alternately with beef cubes, green pepper, and mushroom caps. End with cherry tomato. Sprinkle Brown 'n Season evenly and generously over all surfaces of the meat and vegetables. Use no salt. Heat oil in skillet to sizzling; quickly pan-fry skewers for 10 to 12 minutes, basting once with prepared mustard. *Makes 4 servings. Serve with:* brown rice and red and white cabbage slaw.

Steak On A Stick

1½ pounds of beef
sirloin
½ cup dry sherry
2 tablespoons soy
sauce
1 tablespoon honey
1 tablespoon catchup
1 tablespoon garlic-fla-
vored wine vinegar

Cut beef into 1-inch chunks. Combine remaining ingredients, mixing well. Pour over beef and marinate for ½ hour. Thread beef onto skewers. Grill 4 inches above coals for 15 minutes or to desired doneness. Turn often and baste with marinade. *Makes 6 servings. Serve with:* corn on the cob, pickled beets and a green salad.

Steak And Apple Kebobs

3 pounds top round, ½ inch thick
Red Wine Marinade*

2 large green peppers, cut into 1½-inch squares
4 baking apples, cut into sixths

Cut beef into 1½-inch squares; cover with Red Wine Marinade; refrigerate for at least 12 hours, turning meat cubes several times. Drain, saving marinade. Alternate beef cubes, green pepper squares and apple slices on skewers, using 3 squares of meat to 1 each of peppers and apples. Brush with marinade. Grill 4 inches above coals for 20 to 25 minutes, turning often and basting with marinade. *Makes 6 servings. Serve with*: frozen, stuffed baked potatoes heated on grill, Italian green beans and wedges of iceberg lettuce with Russian dressing.

*Red Wine Marinade

½ cup vegetable oil
¼ cup soy sauce
½ cup dry red wine
1½ teaspoons ground ginger

2 garlic cloves, minced
1 tablespoon curry powder
2 tablespoons catchup
½ teaspoon Tabasco

Combine all ingredients; beat with electric or rotary egg beater until smooth.

Steak And Mushroom Kebobs

2 **pounds sirloin steak,** ¾ **cup vegetable oil**
   cut 1 inch thick ½ **cup wine vinegar**
1 **Bermuda onion,** 1 **teaspoon sugar**
   chopped 12 **medium mushroom**
1 **garlic clove, crushed** **crowns**
1 **teaspoon celery salt**

Cut steak into 1-inch cubes. Combine all remaining ingredients except mushrooms; pour over steak. Chill
until ready to cook. Drain steak, saving sauce. Thread
steak and mushrooms onto skewers. Brush with sauce.
Grill 4 inches above coals, turning often and brushing
with sauce, for about 12 minutes. Serve any remaining
sauce with kebobs. *Makes 6 servings. Serve with*: potato chips, corn on the cob and sliced tomatoes in
French dressing.

Beef En Brochette

1½ **pounds beef filet** **Pepper**
   or **sirloin** 4 **strips bacon**
Salt

Cut beef into 1½-inch cubes, trimming off excess fat.
Sprinkle meat with salt and pepper. Thread onto
skewers, weaving bacon strips around beef. Broil
about 3 inches from heat, turning to brown all sides,
to desired degree of doneness. *Makes 4 servings.*
Serve with: baked potatoes with dairy sour cream
and chives, and a salad of artichoke hearts and chicory.

Stuffed Brochette Of Beef Scallops

1½ **pounds eye of** 1 **can (1 lb.) sauerkraut**
   round, thinly sliced ¼ **teaspoon caraway seed**
   into 18 scallops 3 **tablespoons vege-**
Instant, seasoned meat **table oil**
   tenderizer

Prepare all surfaces of meat, one side at a time as fol-
lows: Moisten meat thoroughly with water, using

pastry brush. Sprinkle meat tenderizer evenly, like salt, over entire surface of meat. Use no salt. To insure penetration and to retain meat juices, pierce meat deeply with kitchen fork at approximately ½-inch intervals. Drain sauerkraut well; add caraway seed and blend. Divide into 18 portions. Wrap each portion of kraut tightly in scallop; secure with wooden pick or tie with string. Lace 3 stuffed scallops onto each of 6 8-to 10-inch metal skewers. *To Broil:* Brush skewered scallops with oil; place on broiler rack 3 inches from heat source; broil for 6 to 8 minutes turning once. *To Grill:* Brush skewered scallops with oil; place on grill set 2 to 3 inches above hot coals. Grill for 6 to 8 minutes, turning frequently. *Makes 6 servings. Serve with:* home-fried potatoes, chilled Italian green beans in French dressing and carrot sticks.

Kebobs Teriyaki

2 **cans (20 oz. each) pineapple chunks**	**Teriyaki Sauce* Ac'cent**
2 **pounds tender, lean beef**	16 **large stuffed olives**

Drain pineapple; save syrup for sauce. Cut beef into cubes a little larger than pineapple chunks. Marinate in Teriyaki Sauce for 2 hours. Drain, saving sauce. Alternate meat and pineapple cubes on 16 skewers, ending each with an olive. Sprinkle with Ac'cent. Broil or grill 4 inches from heat for about 12 minutes, turning often and brushing with sauce. *Makes 8 servings. Serve with:* rice and a tossed salad.

Teriyaki Sauce

1 **cup pineapple syrup**	2 **garlic cloves, minced**
½ **cup soy sauce**	1½ **teaspoons ground ginger**

Combine all ingredients; mix well.

West Indian Skewered Beef

4 small onions, finely chopped
Dash cayenne
2 garlic cloves, minced
1 tablespoon dark brown sugar
1 teaspoon lime juice
2 teaspoons curry powder
½ teaspoon ground cloves
½ teaspoon ground ginger
3 tablespoons warm water
3 tablespoons soy sauce
1½ pounds round steak, cut into ¾-inch cubes

Combine onions, cayenne, garlic, brown sugar, lime juice, curry powder, cloves, and ginger. Blend well. Combine water and soy sauce; blend with spice mixture. Add meat; stir thoroughly with fork. Chill for 6 hours. Drain meat, saving marinade. Thread 5 or 6 pieces of meat onto each skewer. Broil with skewers 3 inches below heat for 15 to 20 minutes, turning frequently and brushing meat with remaining sauce. *Makes 4 to 5 servings. Serve with:* Peanut Sauce*, rice and a salad of garden vegetables.

*Peanut Sauce

2 tablespoons grated onion
2 tablespoons vegetable oil
1 tablespoon dark brown sugar
1 teaspoon lime juice
¼ cup peanut butter
1 cup water
Dash of salt

Sauté onions in oil 5 to 10 minutes until clear. Add brown sugar, lime juice, peanut butter. Blend well. Gradually add water, stirring constantly. Add salt. Cook slowly until sauce is thick and smooth. *Makes 1¼ cups.*

LAMB

Lamb Kebobs

For each skewer you will need 3 2-inch cubes lean lamb, 2 slices of green pepper, 2 mushrooms, 2 squares of bacon, and 2 small onion quarters. Marinate the lamb in Coffee Barbecue Sauce* for several hours. Drain; save marinade. String ingredients onto skewers, beginning and ending with lamb. Brush with sauce; place on grill about 4 inches above coals. Grill for 15 to 20 minutes, turning often and brushing with sauce each time. Slide off skewers onto plates. *Serve with:* potato cakes, mixed vegetables and a watercress and avocado salad.

*Coffee Barbecue Sauce

1 cup vegetable oil	⅛ teaspoon garlic powder
⅓ cup strong cold coffee	¼ cup sugar
2 tablespoons dry red wine	Dash Tabasco
1 tablespoon wine vinegar	1 teaspoon Worcestershire sauce

Combine all ingredients; beat with rotary egg beater or electric blender until thoroughly mixed. *Makes about 1⅔ cups.*

Spicy Lamb Kebobs

2 pounds boneless lamb
1 large onion, minced
1 garlic clove, crushed
½ teaspoon coarsely ground black pepper
1 tablespoon cumin
1 teaspoon ground cardamom
1 teaspoon chili powder
½ teaspoon ground ginger
2 teaspoons salt
1 teaspoon Ac'cent
1 cup dry white wine
⅓ cup vegetable oil

Cut lamb into 1½-inch cubes. Combine remaining ingredients; pour over lamb. Refrigerate for several hours, turning lamb occasionally. Drain lamb, saving marinade. Thread lamb onto skewers; brush with marinade. Grill 4 inches above coals for about 20 minutes, turning often and brushing with marinade. *Makes 4 to 6 servings. Serve with:* herbed rice, summer squash and raw vegetable relishes.

Savory Lamb Kebobs

2 pounds lean, boneless lamb
1 cup dry red wine
¼ cup tarragon vinegar
¾ cup vegetable oil
1 teaspoon salt
1 medium onion, sliced
1 teaspoon leaf marjoram, crumbled
1 teaspoon leaf basil, crumbled
4 small white onions, parboiled
4 (1½ inch) squares green pepper
4 cherry tomatoes

Cut lamb into 12 1½-inch cubes. Combine next 7 ingredients; pour over lamb. Refrigerate for several hours. Drain lamb, saving marinade. On each of 4 skewers, thread 3 cubes of lamb, 1 onion and 1 square of green pepper. Broil or grill for about 15 minutes, turning often and basting with marinade. During last 5 minutes, thread a cherry tomato onto end of each skewer. *Makes 4 servings. Serve with:* buttered green noodles, carrot circles and a tossed salad.

Savory Skewered Lamb

3 pounds lean, bone-less lamb
1 cup dry sherry
⅓ cup vegetable oil
1 teaspoon salt
Dash Tabasco
½ teaspoon thyme
½ teaspoon caraway seed

1 tablespoon snipped parsley
2 garlic cloves, sliced
2 bay leaves, crumbled
1 can (1 lb.) small white potatoes
3 firm medium toma-toes, quartered

Cut lamb into 1½-inch chunks. Combine next 9 ingredients; pour over lamb. Let stand for several hours. Drain, saving marinade. Thread lamb, potatoes and tomatoes onto long skewers. Grill 4 inches above coals for about 15 minutes, turning often and brushing with marinade. *Makes 6 servings. Serve with:* roasted corn on the cob, sliced cucumbers dressed with sour cream and fresh dill, and raw carrot sticks.

Fruited Lamb Kebobs

2 pounds lean, bone-less lamb
Celery
1 cup pineapple juice
½ cup white wine

½ teaspoon rosemary
1 can (1 lb.) pineapple chunks
4 bananas, cut into 1½-inch slices

Cut lamb into 1½-inch pieces. Slice an equal number of celery pieces cut into 1½-inch lengths. Combine pineapple juice, wine and rosemary; pour over lamb and celery. Let stand for at least 1 hour, turning meat occasionally. Drain, saving marinade. Alternate meat, celery, pineapple chunks and bananas on long skewers. Grill 4 inches above coals for about 15 minutes, turning frequently and basting with marinade. *Makes 4 to 6 servings. Serve with:* parslied rice and green beans vinaigrette.

Skewered Lamb And Bacon

1½ pounds boned
lamb shoulder
1 garlic clove
½ cup vegetable oil
¼ cup vinegar

1 teaspoon dry
mustard
1 teaspoon Worcester-
shire sauce
⅛ teaspoon Tabasco
4 strips bacon

Cut lamb into 1½-inch cubes. Rub bowl with slashed garlic clove. Leave garlic in bowl. Blend oil, vinegar and seasonings in bowl with garlic. Add lamb cubes. Chill for several hours or overnight. Drain. Cut bacon strips into fourths. Alternate lamb and bacon on 4 skewers. Broil with surface of meat about 3 inches below source of heat for about 20 minutes. Turn frequently for even browning. *Makes 4 servings. Serve with:* creamed potatoes, green peas and raw vegetable relishes.

Apricot Lamb Kebobs

1½ pounds boneless
shoulder of lamb
12 large dried
apricots
1 can (1 lb.) white
potatoes, drained
3 tablespoons melted
butter *or*
margarine

1 tablespoon
snipped parsley
¼ teaspoon dry
mustard
1 teaspoon salt
¼ teaspoon pepper
⅛ teaspoon garlic salt
⅛ teaspoon onion salt

Cut lamb into 1½-inch cubes. Cook apricots until barely tender. Thread lamb, apricots and potatoes onto 4 skewers. Combine remaining ingredients; mix well. Brush kebobs with this mixture. Grill 4 inches above coals for 15 to 20 minutes, turning often and basting with butter mixture. *Makes 4 servings. Serve with:* mint sauce, canned, fried noodles heated on the grill, and buttered lima beans.

Lamb Kebobs With Fruits

2 pounds boneless lamb
16 pineapple chunks
2 large apples, cut into eighths
16 preserved kumquats
16 maraschino cherries
¼ cup butter or margarine, melted
½ teaspoon salt
½ teaspoon paprika

Cut lamb into 1-inch cubes. On each of 8 skewers alternate lamb cubes, 2 pineapple chunks, 2 apple slices, 2 kumquats and 2 maraschino cherries. Combine melted butter, salt and paprika; blend well; brush skewered foods with this mixture. Grill 4 inches above coals for about 15 minutes, turning often and brushing with butter mixture. *Makes 4 servings (2 skewers per person). Serve with:* hot, buttered French bread, lattice potatoes and a green salad.

Lamb With Spicy Fruit Kebobs

2 pounds boneless lamb, cut into 1½-inch cubes
4 firm bananas, cut into 1-inch slices
1 can (1 lb. 13 oz.) small peach halves
1 pkg. (8 oz.) pitted dates
3 tablespoons melted butter or margarine
1 tablespoon lemon juice
1 teaspoon sugar
1 teaspoon cinnamon
¼ teaspoon ground cloves

Thread lamb onto 4 skewers. Brush bananas with syrup from peaches. Thread fruits onto additional skewers, using 1 peach half, 3 banana slices, and 3 dates on each. Combine remaining ingredients; mix thoroughly. Grill lamb 4 inches above coals for about 7 minutes; turn. Add fruit skewers; brush with butter sauce; cook for 5 to 7 minutes longer, turning once and brushing often with sauce. *Makes 4 servings. Serve with:* buttered noodles, and a salad of endive or celery stuffed with pimiento cheese spread.

Minted Lamb Kebobs

1½ pounds boneless, lean lamb
⅓ cup lemon juice
⅓ cup vegetable oil
1 garlic clove, crushed
1 teaspoon salt
¼ teaspoon coarse black pepper
¼ cup chopped fresh mint leaves

Cut lamb into 1½-inch cubes. Combine remaining ingredients; pour over lamb. Let stand at room temperature for 1 hour. Drain meat, saving marinade. Thread meat onto skewers. Broil or grill 4 inches from source of heat until browned outside and slightly pink inside (about 10 to 12 minutes). Turn often and brush with marinade. Slide off skewers into toasted frankfurter rolls. *Makes 4 servings. Serve with:* a salad of mixed cooked vegetables and potato chips.

Pickle Lamb Kebobs

½ cup liquid from sweet gherkins
½ cup catchup
½ cup water
6 whole cloves
1 bay leaf
1 teaspoon instant minced onion flakes
1 teaspoon salt
½ teaspoon peppercorns
1½ pounds boned shoulder *or* leg of lamb, cut into 1½-inch cubes
1 medium eggplant, cut into ½-inch thick slices
12 sweet gherkins
1 medium pineapple, cut into wedges

Combine pickle liquid, catchup, water and seasonings. Add lamb. Marinate for several hours or overnight. Put lamb onto skewers. Broil 5 to 6 inches from source of heat, or cook on outdoor grill for 10 to 12 minutes per side, brushing frequently with marinade. Put eggplant onto skewers. Grill for 8 to 10 minutes per side, brushing frequently with marinade. Put pickles and pineapple onto skewers. Grill for 5 minutes per side, brushing frequently with marinade. *Makes 4 to 6 servings. Serve with:* rice and a salad of garden vegetables.

Ground Lamb Kebobs

1½ **pounds lean, ground lamb**
3 **tablespoons rolled oats**
3 **tablespoons tomato paste**
3 **tablespoons finely chopped onions**
2 **teaspoons salt**
⅛ **teaspoon pepper**
¼ **teaspoon ground cardamom**

Combine all ingredients; mix thoroughly. Shape into small balls about 1½ inches in diameter. Chill until firm. Thread onto skewers. Grill 3 inches above coals, turning often to brown on all sides. *Makes 4 to 5 servings. Serve with:* minted new potatoes, green peas with mushrooms and endive salad.

Lamb And Vegetable Kebobs

2 **pounds boneless lamb, cut into 1-inch cubes**
2 **medium zucchini, sliced and parboiled**
1½ **cups cauliflower flowerettes, parboiled**
12 **canned baby carrots**
12 **small canned white potatoes**
Paprika
⅓ **cup catchup**
1 **tablespoon prepared mustard**
3 **tablespoons vegetable oil**

Thread lamb and vegetables onto 6 long skewers. Sprinkle cauliflower and potatoes with paprika. Combine last 3 ingredients; mix well; brush on skewered foods. Grill 4 inches above coals for about 15 minutes, turning often and basting with catchup mixture. *Makes 6 servings. Serve with:* hot club rolls and a tossed salad.

Lamb And Eggplant Kebobs

12 1-inch cubes lean lamb (about 1 lb.)	**1 green pepper, cut into 1-inch squares**
4 small onions, halved	**1 small eggplant, cut into chunks**
4 medium mushrooms	**French dressing**

Marinate meat and vegetables in French dressing for at least 1 hour. Drain, saving marinade. Thread 4 skewers, beginning and ending with meat. Broil or grill about 4 inches from source of heat for 20 to 25 minutes, turning often and basting with marinade. *Makes 4 servings. Serve with:* baked potatoes, grilled tomato halves and a tossed green salad.

Kebobs—Mediterranean Style

1 can (8 oz.) tomato sauce	**1 teaspoon crushed oregano**
½ cup orange juice	**1 garlic clove, crushed**
¼ cup mint *or* red currant jelly	**2 pounds boneless lamb, cut into 1-inch cubes**
¼ cup vegetable oil	**3 zucchini, cut into ½-inch slices**
2 teaspoons instant minced onion	**1 large unpeeled orange, cut into 6 wedges**
1 teaspoon salt	

Combine tomato sauce, orange juice, jelly, oil, onion, salt, oregano and garlic in small saucepan; heat until jelly melts. Place meat in shallow nonmetal pan; pour tomato sauce mixture over. Cover; refrigerate for several hours, turning meat occasionally. Drain meat, reserving marinade. On 6 12-inch skewers alternate meat and zucchini, beginning and ending with meat. Grill 5 inches above coals for about 30 minutes, turning and basting frequently with marinade. During last 5 minutes of cooking, put orange wedges onto ends of skewers; baste with sauce; continue grilling until heated. *Makes 6 servings. Serve with:* thin spaghetti in butter sauce, Italian green beans and cucumber and onion ring salad.

Lamb, Corn And Tomato Kebobs

1 cup vegetable oil	¼ teaspoon coarsely
½ cup lemon juice	ground black pepper
2 garlic cloves,	3 pounds boneless
crushed	lamb
1 tablespoon salt	8 cherry tomatoes
2 teaspoons dried	4 ears of corn, cut
dill weed	crosswise into
	2-inch pieces

Combine first 6 ingredients; mix well. Cut lamb into 1- to 1½-inch cubes; pour marinade over cubes. Chill for 4 hours, turning meat occasionally. Drain meat, saving marinade. Thread meat, tomatoes and corn onto skewers, beginning and ending with meat. Brush with marinade. Grill 4 inches above coals for 15 to 20 minutes, turning once and basting with marinade. To serve, slip food off skewers onto plates. *Makes 8 servings. Serve with:* French fried potatoes and tossed salad.

Kebobs Burgundy

1 small leg of lamb	¼ cup lemon juice
(about 6 lbs.)	½ Bermuda onion,
2 cups Burgundy	finely chopped
2 cups vegetable oil	Salt and pepper to taste

Bone lamb; cut into 1½-inch cubes. Combine remaining ingredients; pour over lamb in deep glass or earthenware bowl. Refrigerate for 3 days, turning meat occasionally. Drain lamb, saving marinade. Thread 6 cubes of lamb onto each skewer, brush with marinade. Grill 4 inches above coals, turning often and brushing with marinade, for 15 to 20 minutes. *Makes 6 servings. Serve with:* curried rice, green peas with onions and a Waldorf salad.

Lamb Kebobs A L'Orange

½ cup firmly packed brown sugar
1 teaspoon dry mustard
¼ teaspoon allspice
1 tablespoon instant minced onion
2 tablespoons lime juice
2 cans or jars (11 oz. each) mandarin oranges
2 pounds lean lamb
Pitted ripe olives

Combine first 5 ingredients. Add syrup from oranges. Stir until sugar dissolves. Cut lamb into 1½-inch cubes; cover with first mixture. Chill for several hours. When ready to cook, drain lamb, saving marinade. Thread lamb, orange sections and olives onto skewers. Brush with marinade. Grill 4 inches above heat for about 20 minutes, turning several times and basting with marinade. *Makes 4 servings. Serve with:* corn on the cob, hot buttered French bread, and raw vegetable relishes.

Greek Kebobs

1 leg of lamb, boned
1 cup vegetable oil
⅓ cup lemon juice
⅔ cup dry white wine
2 garlic cloves, minced
2 teaspoons oregano
1 teaspoon salt
¼ teaspoon pepper
2 bay leaves
4 tomatoes, quartered
2 medium onions, quartered and separated
2 green peppers, cut into 1-inch squares

Cut lamb into 1½-inch cubes. Combine next 8 ingredients; pour over lamb. Place tomatoes and onions on top. Cover; refrigerate for several hours. Thread lamb, tomatoes, green peppers and onions onto skewers. Brush with marinade. Grill 4 inches above coals for about 20 minutes, turning often and basting with marinade. *Makes 8 servings. Serve with:* rice pilaf, broccoli, artichoke hearts and carrot sticks.

Lamb Kebobs Milano

2 pounds lean lamb   16 pitted black olives
1 can (1 lb.) small   Chianti Sauce*
   white onions

Cut lamb into 1½-inch cubes. Alternate lamb cubes, onions and olives on 8 skewers, using 2 olives per skewer. Brush with Chianti Sauce. Grill 4 inches above heat for about 20 minutes, turning several times and brushing with sauce. *Makes 4 servings. Serve with:* spaghetti dressed with butter and grated Parmesan cheese, and broccoli. Add a salad of Romaine and chicory.

*Chianti Sauce

⅓ cup Chianti   ½ teaspoon oregano
   wine   Dash of sugar
¼ cup vegetable oil   Salt and pepper to taste

Combine all ingredients. Mix well.

Lamb Shish Kebob

1 shoulder of lamb   ¼ teaspoon salt
½ cup Burgundy   ⅛ teaspoon pepper
2 teaspoons dried   ¼ cup vegetable oil
   tarragon

Have shoulder boned at market. Cut into 2-inch cubes, removing any excess fat. Combine remaining ingredients; pour over lamb. Marinate in refrigerator for several hours or overnight. Drain, saving marinade. String lamb onto long skewers. Grill slowly over hot coals to desired degree of doneness, with meat 3 or 4 inches above heat, basting occasionally with heated marinade. *Makes 8 to 10 servings. Serve with:* brown rice, buttered zucchini and a tomato salad.

Lamb En Brochette

4 tablespoons vege-
table oil
⅓ cup soy sauce
¼ teaspoon Tabasco
1 large onion,
finely grated

3 tablespoons lemon
juice
1 teaspoon salt
1 teaspoon sugar
3 pounds lean lamb

Combine all ingredients except lamb; mix thorough-ly. Cut lamb into 1½-inch cubes and drop into the marinade. Let stand for at least 1 hour, turning often. Thread lamb cubes onto skewers. Broil or grill 4 inches from source of heat until lamb reaches de-sired degree of doneness (about 20 minutes), turning often and basting often with marinade. *Makes 6 serv-ings. Serve with:* a salad of fresh vegetables, potato chips and hot club rolls.

Note: Where available, sprigs of fresh rosemary, threaded between lamb cubes, impart a delicious flavor.

Oriental Kebobs

2 pounds lean lamb
2 large onions
1 small eggplant

2 green peppers
1 box cherry tomatoes
Marinade Rosé*

Cut lamb into 1½-inch cubes. Cut onions into sixths, eggplant into 1-inch cubes and green peppers into 1-inch pieces. Thread with tomatoes onto skewers. Place filled skewers on long strips of heavy-duty alu-minum foil about 6 inches wide. Brush liberally with marinade. When ready to cook, remove from foil; save foil. Place on grill 4 inches above coals. Brown quickly, turning twice. Return each kebob to foil. Spoon remaining marinade over them. Seal foil; re-turn to grill. Cook for ½ hour without turning. *Makes 6 servings. Serve with:* curried rice and a tossed salad.

*Marinade Rosé

1 medium onion, minced	2 teaspoons sugar
¼ cup vegetable oil	1 teaspoon rosemary
1 tablespoon lemon juice	1 teaspoon chervil
½ cup rosé wine	¾ teaspoon salt
	⅛ teaspoon pepper

Cook onions in oil until soft but not brown. Add remaining ingredients; mix well. *Makes about 1 cup.*

Skewered Lamb Teriyaki

½ cup pineapple juice	¼ teaspoon ground ginger
¼ cup soy sauce	½ teaspoon Ac'cent
2 teaspoons brown sugar	⅛ teaspoon thyme
½ teaspoon Worcestershire sauce	1 pound boned lamb shoulder
½ small garlic clove, minced	6 bacon strips
	8 mushroom caps
	8 pineapple chunks

Combine first 8 ingredients; mix well. Cut lamb into 12 cubes. Cut bacon strips into halves; fold each piece in two. On each of 4 long skewers, string 3 pieces of lamb, 3 bacon folds, 2 mushroom caps and 2 pineapple chunks, beginning and ending with lamb. Place in shallow pan; pour pineapple juice mixture over. Chill for several hours. Drain, saving sauce. Broil for 10 minutes, with surface of meat 3 inches below heat; brush twice with sauce. Turn, broil for 10 minutes longer, brushing twice with sauce. Serve on rice; heat any remaining sauce; pour over all. *Makes 4 servings. Serve with:* a salad of garden vegetables.

Chelo Kebobs

1 package instant meat marinade
⅔ cup dry sherry
1 teaspoon mint flakes
½ teaspoon marjoram
3 pounds boneless lamb shoulder, cut into 1½-inch cubes

1 small eggplant, cut into 1½-inch cubes
2 medium green peppers, cut into 1½-inch squares
1 can (1 lb.) white onions
2 tablespoons vegetable oil
6 cherry tomatoes

Blend instant meat marinade and sherry in a small bowl; add mint and marjoram; blend thoroughly. Pour marinade over cubed meat in shallow pan. Pierce all surfaces thoroughly with fork; add eggplant. Marinate for 15 minutes, turning several times. Remove meat and eggplant from marinade; drain well, saving marinade. Lace meat onto 6 12-inch metal skewers alternating with eggplant, green peppers and onions. Add oil to reserved marinade and use for brushing skewers during cooking. Place skewers on grill, set 3 to 4 inches above coals; grill for 15 to 20 minutes, turning and brushing frequently with marinade. Put cherry tomato onto each skewer during last 3 to 4 minutes of cooking. *Makes 6 servings. Serve with:* curried rice, green beans and a tossed salad.

Lamb Saté

2 garlic cloves, minced
2 medium onions, finely chopped
¼ cup peanut butter
2 tablespoons brown sugar

¼ teaspoon Tabasco
¼ cup soy sauce
3 tablespoons lime juice
2 pounds boneless lamb, cut into 1-inch cubes

Combine all ingredients except lamb; mix well; pour over lamb. Chill for several hours. Drain lamb; save marinade. Thread lamb onto skewers; brush with marinade. Grill 3 inches above coals for 20 minutes, turning once and brushing often with marinade. *Makes 4 or 5 servings. Serve with:* curried rice, eggplant sauté and a crisp green salad.

Curried Lamb Kebobs

1 tablespoon curry powder
1 cup applesauce
1 teaspoon salt
⅛ teaspoon Tabasco
2 tablespoons lime juice
1 teaspoon sugar
2 pounds boneless lamb, cut into 1-inch cubes

Stir curry powder into applesauce, mixing thoroughly. Add all remaining ingredients except lamb. Pour applesauce mixture over lamb. Chill for several hours. Thread lamb onto skewers; brush with marinade. Grill 4 inches above coals for about 20 minutes, turning often and brushing with marinade. *Makes 6 servings. Serve with:* rice, buttered zucchini and a salad of sliced tomatoes, cucumbers and onion rings.

Lamb And Onion Shish Kebobs

20 cubes of lean lamb
8 small onions, halved
½ teaspoon peppercorns
1 teaspoon salt
Melted butter or margarine
Worcestershire sauce

Thread 4 skewers, using 5 cubes of lamb and 4 onion halves on each, beginning and ending with lamb. Crush peppercorns with salt, using mortar and pestle. Sprinkle skewers with this mixture. Let stand for 15 to 20 minutes. Broil or grill about 4 inches from heat for 15 to 20 minutes or until browned. Turn often and brush with melted butter to which a little Worcestershire sauce has been added. *Makes 4 servings. Serve with:* fluffy rice and eggplant in Creole sauce.

East Indian Kebobs

2 pounds boneless
lamb
¾ cup yogurt
1 teaspoon pow-
dered ginger
¼ teaspoon
Tabasco
2 teaspoons pow-
dered coriander

¼ teaspoon pow-
dered cloves
½ teaspoon powdered
cinnamon
¼ teaspoon turmeric
1 medium onion,
minced
2 teaspoons lime juice
Salt and sugar to taste

Cut lamb into 1½-inch cubes. Combine remaining ingredients; pour over lamb. Marinate for 3 hours; drain lamb, saving marinade. Thread lamb onto skewers. Brush with marinade. Grill 4 inches above coals for about 20 minutes, turning often and brushing with marinade. *Makes 4 to 6 servings. Serve with:* rice, buttered eggplant and a cucumber, avocado and onion ring salad.

Armenian Shish Kebobs

1½ pounds boned,
lean lamb
3 tablespoons
tomato paste
3 tablespoons
minced onion
2 teaspoons
lemon juice

2 teaspoons salt
¼ teaspoon allspice
Few grains coarsely
ground black pepper
½ pound eggplant
Tomato sauce

Cut lamb into 1¼-inch chunks. Add next 6 ingredients; mix thoroughly. Refrigerate for several hours. Cut unpeeled eggplant into chunks the same size as the lamb. Alternate lamb and eggplant on skewers using 2 chunks of lamb to 1 of eggplant. Broil 4 inches above coals for about 15 minutes, turning to brown on all sides. *Makes 3 to 4 servings. Serve with:* any favorite tomato sauce, rice pilaf and spinach salad.

Ground Lamb Shish Kebobs

2 pounds lean
lamb, ground
⅓ cup wheat germ
⅓ cup minced
onion
⅓ cup minced
parsley

¼ teaspoon coarsely
ground black pepper
¾ teaspoon salt
Melted butter *or*
margarine

Combine all ingredients. Shape into 12 thick "sausages." Thread 3 onto each skewer, leaving at least ½ inch between "sausages." Brush with melted butter or margarine. Broil 4 inches from source of heat for 15 to 20 minutes, turning often and brushing with melted butter. *Makes 4 to 6 servings. Serve with:* kasha (buckwheat groats) or brown rice and green peas with mushrooms.

Lamb Shashlik

2 pounds boned
lamb shoulder
1 garlic clove
½ cup vegetable oil
¼ cup vinegar
1 teaspoon Ac'cent

1 teaspoon dry mustard
1 teaspoon Worcester-
shire sauce
Dash cayenne
Few drops Tabasco

Cut lamb into 1-inch cubes. Rub bowl with slashed garlic clove; leave in bowl. Add remaining ingredients; mix well. Add lamb cubes; chill for several hours, turning occasionally. Drain. String onto skewers; broil for 20 minutes, turning to brown. *Makes 4 servings. Serve with:* kasha (buckwheat groats), pickled beets and a crisp salad.

Shashlik Caucasian I

Leg of baby lamb
  (about 6 lbs.)
2 cups Burgundy
2 cups vegetable oil
Juice of 2 lemons

Salt and pepper
½ Bermuda onion,
  finely chopped
Vegetables, as desired

Cut lamb into 2-inch squares. Combine Burgundy, oil, lemon juice, seasonings, onion. Place mixture in earthenware crock or in deep china or glass dish; do not use metal. Marinate for 3 days in refrigerator. When ready to cook, use 12-inch skewers. On each skewer alternate pieces of lamb with ⅓ tomato, ⅓-inch slice of onion (1 inch in diameter) and a square of green pepper, if desired. Each 12-inch skewer will take about 5 cubes of lamb, 2 tomatoes, and 2 onion slices. Broil on both sides gently for about 8 minutes on each side, depending on thickness of meat. If possible, finish off in a 350° oven for 10 minutes.

For indoor service, make this quick, appetizing sauce: blend ¼ cup Burgundy or tarragon vinegar with 2 to 3 tablespoons melted, warm butter or margarine; pour over each serving as a sauce. *Serve with:* hot steamed rice and a green vegetable or tossed salad.

Shashlik Caucasian II

2 pounds boneless
  lamb
1 large onion,
  minced
1 tablespoon
  vegetable oil
1 teaspoon salt
¼ teaspoon coarsely
  ground black
  pepper

1 tablespoon lemon
  juice
¼ cup dry red wine
2 medium onions, cut
  into chunks
Brandy for flaming, if
  desired

Cut lamb into 1½-inch cubes. Combine next 6 ingredients; pour over lamb. Marinate for several hours, turning lamb several times. Thread lamb and onion chunks alternately onto skewers. Grill 4 inches above coals for 10 to 15 minutes, turning often and brushing with marinade. Flame with warmed brandy if desired. *Makes 4 servings. Serve with:* kasha (buckwheat groats), pickled beets, scallions and a salad of green beans.

Ranch Kebobs

Cut lamb into 1½-inch cubes. Cover with Garlic Marinade*; let stand for 1 hour. Drain lamb, saving marinade; wrap each cube in bacon. Thread skewers with lamb cubes, parboiled small, white onions, pitted ripe olives and squares of green pepper. Grill 4 inches above coals for 15 minutes; turn; grill for 15 minutes longer. Brush frequently with marinade during broiling. *Serve with:* canned spaghetti in tomato sauce and a salad of raw cauliflower and cooked green peas.

*Garlic Marinade

1 **cup hot water**	2 **tablespoons lemon**
⅓ **cup soy sauce**	**juice**
¼ **cup honey**	¼ **teaspoon salt**
2 **tablespoons vege-**	4 **garlic cloves,**
table oil	**crushed**

Combine all ingredients; mix well. *Makes about 1¾ cups.*

Turkish Sis Kebabi

1 large onion,
   chopped
2 tablespoons
   olive oil
¼ cup lemon
   juice
1 tablespoon salt

½ teaspoon freshly
   ground black
   pepper
2 pounds lean, bone-
   less lamb
2 tablespoons whip-
   ping cream

Place the onion in a deep bowl; sprinkle with oil, lemon juice, salt and pepper. Trim any excess fat from lamb; cut into 1½-inch cubes. Add to onion mixture; turn to coat well. Chill for 4 hours, turning occasionally. Thread lamb onto 4 long skewers; brush evenly with cream. Grill or broil 4 inches from heat for about 15 minutes. Slip meat off skewers onto serving plates. *Makes 4 servings. Serve with:* rice, grilled tomato halves and fried eggplant.

Shashlik

2 pounds boned
   lamb shoulder
Juice of 2 lemons
½ cup finely
   chopped parsley

1 teaspoon dried dill
1 garlic clove, slashed
Salt and pepper

Cut lamb into 1½-inch cubes; put in deep bowl. Combine remaining ingredients; pour over lamb. Chill for several hours. Drain lamb. Run skewers through lamb cubes; grill 4 inches above coals, turning often and brushing with marinade. Cook evenly for about 20 minutes or to desired degree of doneness. *Makes 4 servings. Serve with:* yellow (saffron) rice, sweet-sour cucumber slices and onion rings, and tossed salad.

PORK

Baked Pork Kebobs

- **3** pounds boneless pork shoulder
- **½** cup honey
- **1** tablespoon grated lemon peel
- **3** tablespoons lemon juice
- **⅓** cup water
- **2** tablespoons catchup
- **1½** teaspoons salt
- **¼** teaspoon pepper
- **¼** teaspoon ground cinnamon
- **½** teaspoon ground ginger
- **1** small onion, minced
- **½** pound large dried apricots
- **½** pound large dried pitted prunes

Cut pork into 1½-inch squares. Combine all remaining ingredients except apricots and prunes; pour over pork. Let stand for several hours, turning pork often. Drain pork; place in roasting pan; baste with marinade. Bake at 350° for 1 hour, basting often. Meanwhile cover prunes and apricots with water; bring to boil; drain. Cool pork and fruits enough to handle. Thread alternately onto 6 long skewers. Brush with marinade. Broil 4 inches below heat until lightly browned. *Makes 6 servings. Serve with:* mashed yams, green beans with almonds and a salad of Romaine.

Curried Pork Kebobs

2 pounds lean, bone-
less pork
2 garlic cloves,
minced
⅓ cup butter *or*
margarine, melted
1 can (8 oz.) tomato
sauce
1 teaspoon turmeric
1 teaspoon salt
½ teaspoon coarsely
ground black pepper
2 teaspoons curry
powder
1 cup dry sherry
1 can (1 lb.) small white
onions, drained

Cut pork into 1-inch cubes. Cook garlic in butter in a large skillet. Add tomato sauce, turmeric, salt, pepper and curry powder; mix well. Stir and simmer for 5 minutes. Add sherry; heat. Pour over pork. Let stand for 2 hours. Drain, saving marinade. Thread pork and onions onto skewers. Brush with marinade. Place in pan on broiler rack. Broil 4 inches below heat until pork is well done, turning several times and basting with marinade. *Makes 4 servings. Serve with:* hashed brown potatoes, applesauce and frozen mixed vegetables. Add a salad of endive with blue cheese dressing.

Sherried Pork Kebobs

2 pounds boneless
pork
1 cup dry sherry
¼ cup soy sauce
1 teaspoon sugar
1 garlic clove, crushed

Cut pork into 1½-inch cubes. Combine remaining ingredients; pour over pork. Marinate for 4 hours, turning pork occasionally. Thread pork onto skewers; brush with marinade. Grill 4 inches above coals for at least 30 minutes, or until pork is thoroughly done, turning often and basting with marinade. *Makes 4 to 6 servings. Serve with:* corn chips, applesauce and sautéed parsnips.

Sweet And Pungent Ham Kebobs

Cut cooked ham into 1½-inch cubes. Alternate on skewers with pineapple chunks, maraschino cherries and cubes of peeled, parboiled eggplant. Brush with Sweet and Pungent Sauce*. Grill 3 inches above coals for 8 to 10 minutes, or until eggplant is tender, turning often and basting with sauce.

*Sweet And Pungent Sauce

3 tablespoons vegetable oil	Syrup from 1-pound can pineapple chunks with enough water to make ⅔ cup
1 teaspoon salt	
½ cup wine vinegar	
1½ teaspoons soy sauce	½ cup firmly packed brown sugar

Combine all ingredients in saucepan. Simmer for 15 minutes, stirring often.

Pork And Apple Kebobs

Cut 2 pounds boneless pork shoulder, into 1½-inch cubes. Cover with Claret Marinade* and refrigerate for 12 hours or longer, turning cubes several times. Drain pork, saving marinade. Alternate cubes of pork and thick slices of apple on skewers. Grill 4 inches above coals, turning often and basting with marinade, until pork is thoroughly done (about 30 minutes). *Makes 4 to 6 servings. Serve with:* scalloped sweet potatoes, cauliflower with chive butter and a green salad.

*Claret Marinade

½ cup vegetable oil	1 tablespoon curry powder
½ cup claret	
2 tablespoons minced candied ginger	¼ teaspoon coarsely ground black pepper
2 garlic cloves, grated	¼ cup soy sauce
	2 tablespoons catchup

Combine all ingredients; mix well.

Fruited Pork Kebobs

Cut boned smoked pork butt into 1½-inch cubes, allowing 3 cubes per skewer. String onto skewers with canned pineapple chunks, preserved kumquats and unpeeled red apple chunks. Place in long, shallow pan or platter. Pour Sauce* over all; marinate for several hours, turning often; drain. Broil with food 4 inches below moderate heat for about 40 minutes, turning, and basting with sauce at frequent intervals. *Serve with:* potatoes au gratin, asparagus and a tossed salad.

*Sauce

½ **cup red currant jelly**	2 **teaspoons prepared**
¼ **cup butter** *or*	**mustard**
margarine	¼ **teaspoon nutmeg**
¼ **cup lemon juice**	1 **teaspoon cinnamon**

Combine all ingredients in small saucepan; stir over low heat until jelly melts and ingredients are well blended.

Skewered Pork With Fruits

Lean boneless *or*	**Apple chunks**
boned pork	**Canned pineapple**
Marinade*	**chunks**
Small white onions	

Cut pork into 1-inch cubes. Cover with marinade; chill for several hours or overnight. Drain; saving marinade. Peel onions; parboil for 5 minutes. To make apple chunks, peel and core firm cooking apples; cut into eighths; cut each eighth in half. String pork cubes, onions and fruit onto long skewers. Brush with marinade. Broil 4 inches below heat for 30 minutes, turning frequently and brushing with marinade. To serve, slide food off skewers. *Serve with:* mashed yams, lima beans and a salad of Romaine.

2 cups canned pine-
  apple juice
¼ cup vegetable oil
2 tablespoons soy
  sauce
1 teaspoon powdered
  ginger

¼ teaspoon powdered
  cloves
½ teaspoon powdered
  cinnamon
2 medium onions,
  sliced
1 tablespoon lime
  juice

Combine all ingredients; mix well.

Cranberry Kebobs

1 small smoked bone-
  less pork butt
2 cups fresh cran-
  berries
1 cup water
¾ cup sugar
1 teaspoon instant
  minced onion

1 tablespoon grated
  lemon peel
1 teaspoon dry
  mustard
18 mushroom caps
18 pineapple chunks

Simmer smoked pork butt in water to cover for about
1 hour; cool; cut into 1½-inch cubes. Meanwhile combine cranberries, water, sugar, onion, lemon peel and
dry mustard; cook over low heat, stirring often, until
thick. String pork cubes, mushrooms and pineapple
chunks onto skewers. Brush with cranberry mixture;
broil with surface of food 4 inches below heat, until
mushrooms are done, turning often and basting with
cranberry mixture. Serve remaining cranberry mixture with finished kebobs. *Makes 6 servings. Serve
with:* baked yams, broccoli and a grated carrot and
raisin salad.

Javanese Kebobs

2 pounds pork tenderloin
1 cup finely chopped onion
2 garlic cloves, minced
2 tablespoons coriander
3 tablespoons brown sugar
¼ cup lime juice
¼ cup soy sauce
¼ cup vegetable oil
1 tablespoon chili powder
4 preserved kumquats

Cut pork into 1-inch cubes. Combine all remaining ingredients except kumquats. Pour over pork; marinate for 2 hours; thread pork cubes onto skewers, ¼ inch apart. Grill 3 inches above coals for about 25 minutes, turning three or four times and brushing with marinade. During last 5 minutes, thread a preserved kumquat onto end of each skewer. *Makes 4 servings. Serve with:* raisin rice, acorn squash (baked in foil on grill) and a crisp salad.

Glazed Smoked Pork Chops With Fruit Kebobs—Polynesian Style

½ cup honey
½ cup lime *or* lemon juice
¼ cup light corn syrup *or* 2 tablespoons sugar
1½ tablespoons soy sauce
½ teaspoon cloves
½ teaspoon grated lime *or* lemon peel, optional
½ teaspoon salt
6 thick (1 to 1¼ inches) smoked pork chops*
2 large oranges, peeled and sliced
½ medium cantaloupe, peeled and seeds removed, cut into chunks
½ medium honeydew melon, peeled and seeds removed, cut into chunks

*If smoked pork chops are not available, fresh pork loin or rib chops may be substituted.

Combine first 7 ingredients in saucepan; mix and heat. Thread chops onto double-pronged kebob skewers. If double-pronged skewers are unavailable, broil chops in greased, hinged rack or directly on greased grill. Grill about 5 inches above coals until well browned on first side (about 15 minutes). Turn; grill until well done (12 to 15 minutes). Brush chops with sauce frequently during grilling. Thread fruit onto double-pronged or single-pronged kebob skewers. Brush with glaze; warm, do not brown, on grill for 3 to 5 minutes. *Makes 6 servings. For hearty eaters allow 2 chops per person. Serve with:* buttered canned yams, green beans with almonds and a tossed salad.

Polynesian Pork Kebobs

1 **jar (8 oz.) red maraschino cherries**	2 **pounds boned pork shoulder, cut into 1-inch cubes**
½ **cup soy sauce**	1 **can (13 or 13¼ oz.) pineapple chunks**
½ **cup honey**	1 **cup pitted dates**
2½ **teaspoons powdered ginger**	1 **cup drained preserved kumquats**

Drain cherries, reserving syrup. Combine cherry syrup, soy sauce, honey and ginger in bowl. Add pork cubes and marinate for 2 or more hours, turning occasionally. Pour off marinade; reserve. Place pork cubes on skewers, leaving about ½-inch space between each. Grill 4 inches above coals for 15 minutes on each side, basting occasionally. Alternate maraschino cherries, pineapple, dates and kumquats on skewers. Brush with marinade; grill for 1 to 2 minutes on each side, or just until fruit is hot. Heat remaining marinade and serve with kebobs. *Makes 6 servings. Serve with:* sliced, fried yams, a green vegetable and an endive salad.

Oriental Pork Kebobs

2 pounds lean, boneless pork
1 teaspoon powdered ginger
½ teaspoon coarsely ground black pepper
3 garlic cloves, minced
½ cup soy sauce
1 can (1 lb.) pineapple chunks
8 preserved kumquats, halved

Cut pork into 1-inch cubes; sprinkle with ginger, pepper and garlic. Pour soy sauce over pork, toss with pork to coat. Refrigerate for 2 hours, turning pork once or twice. Drain, saving marinade. Thread pork, pineapple chunks and halved kumquats alternately onto skewers. Grill 4 inches above coals until pork is well done (about 30 minutes). Turn several times and baste with marinade. *Makes 4 servings. Serve with:* rice, glazed carrots and a green salad.

Pork Saté I

3 pounds pork loin, boned
1 cup thinly sliced onions
½ teaspoon salt
¼ teaspoon pepper
1 tablespoon ground coriander
1 tablespoon cumin seed
2 tablespoons dark brown sugar
¼ cup soy sauce
1 teaspoon Ac'cent
¼ teaspoon powdered ginger
¼ cup lime juice

Remove excess fat from pork; cut into 1-inch cubes. Combine with onions. Combine remaining ingredients; mix well; pour over pork and onions. Refrigerate overnight. Remove pork cubes and string onto 6 skewers, spacing ¼ inch apart. Brush with marinade. Grill 3 inches above coals for about 25 minutes, turning every 5 minutes and brushing with marinade. *Makes 6 servings. Serve with:* curried rice, broccoli and grilled tomatoes.

Pork Saté II

1 tablespoon chili
   powder
1 small onion, chopped
1 tablespoon scraped,
   grated fresh ginger
   root
3 tablespoons lemon
   juice

1 tablespoon salt
¼ cup water
2 pounds boneless
   pork butt
2 tablespoons vege-
   table oil

Combine chili powder, onion, ginger root, lemon juice, salt and water. Blend at high speed for about 30 seconds, or until mixture is smooth. If necessary turn off blender and scrape down, then blend again. Slice pork 1 inch thick, trim off excess fat, cut into ½-inch pieces. Pour blended mixture over pork; stir until evenly coated. Chill for 2 hours, turning occasionally; drain. Thread tightly onto small skewers about 6 inches long. Brush with oil. Broil or grill about 2 inches from heat for at least 10 minutes, or until meat is brown and no pink color shows inside. Serve on skewers, as a first course. *Makes about 24.*

Autumn Kebobs

On skewers alternate cubes of fully cooked ham, pineapple chunks, chunks of partially cooked sweet potatoes (almost done but still firm) and spiced crab apples. Grill 5 inches above glowing coals until potatoes are done and foods are browned (about 20 minutes), turning often and basting with the following sauce: melt ¼ cup butter or margarine; add ⅓ cup brown sugar and ½ cup pineapple syrup from can of pineapple chunks. Bring to boil, stirring until sugar dissolves. Simmer for 5 minutes. *Makes about 1 cup.* *Serve with:* canned Boston-style baked beans, Boston brown bread and butter sandwiches and coleslaw.

Winter Kebobs

1½ pounds ground cooked ham

⅔ cup quick or old-fashioned oats, uncooked

¼ teaspoon pepper

1 teaspoon Worcestershire sauce

2 eggs, beaten

¼ cup milk

18 canned pineapple chunks, drained

6 pieces peeled yellow winter squash, about 2 x 2 x 1 inches each

6 small white onions, peeled

1 medium green pepper, cut into 12 pieces

1 red apple, cored and cut into 6 wedges

French dressing

For ham balls: combine ham, oats, pepper, Worcestershire sauce, eggs and milk. Shape ham mixture around pineapple chunks to form 18 ham balls.

Cook squash pieces and onions in boiling salted water 5 minutes; drain. Alternate 3 ham balls, 1 squash piece, 1 onion, 2 green pepper pieces and 1 apple wedge on 6 12-inch metal skewers. (To be sure that ham balls stay on skewers, thread through pineapple chunks in the center.) Brush kebobs with French dressing. Broil about 6 inches from source of heat for about 8 minutes. Turn; brush again with French dressing; broil for about 5 minutes or until done. *Serve with:* sour cream sauce, made by combining 1 cup dairy sour cream, 2 tablespoons Dijon mustard and ½ teaspoon onion salt. *Makes 6 servings. Serve with:* baked potatoes, carrots and a green salad.

POULTRY

Hibachi Chicken Kebobs

4 whole broiler-fryer
chicken breasts,
uncooked
2 medium zucchini,
cut into ¾-inch
slices
2 green peppers,
cut into pieces about
1½ inches square
16 small white onions,
parboiled for
5 minutes

2 teaspoons salt
1 teaspoon Ac'cent
½ cup butter *or*
margarine, melted
1 tablespoon dried
leaf tarragon
1 tablespoon lemon
juice
2 tomatoes, cut into
8 wedges each

Bone chicken breasts; remove skin. Cut each breast half into 6 to 8 chunks, about 1½ inches square. Alternate chunks on 16 skewers with zucchini, green pepper pieces and onions. Sprinkle with salt and Ac'cent. Combine melted butter, tarragon and lemon juice. Brush over kebobs; grill 3 inches above coals for 5 to 10 minutes. Turn, add tomatoes to ends of skewers and grill for 5 minutes longer, brushing occasionally with butter mixture, until chicken and vegetables are tender. *Makes 8 servings. Serve with:* new potatoes, Brussels sprouts and grilled tomatoes.

Iranian Chicken Kebobs

1 cup finely grated onion	⅛ teaspoon ground saffron**
½ cup lemon juice	1 tablespoon water
2 teaspoons salt	4 tablespoons melted butter *or* margarine
2 broiler chickens (about 2 lbs. each), each cut into 8 pieces*	

* Or buy chicken parts
** If saffron is unavailable use turmeric

Combine onion, lemon juice and salt, blending well. Add chicken pieces and coat well. Chill for 4 hours, turning occasionally. Drain chicken, saving marinade; thread close together on long skewers. Mix saffron and water, add melted butter; brush chicken evenly with butter mixture. Grill or broil about 4 inches from heat for about 30 minutes or until chicken is thoroughly done, turning occasionally and basting with marinade. Remove from skewers onto serving platter. *Makes 4 servings. Serve with:* Chelo (recipe below) and any green vegetable or salad.

Chelo

Cook 2 cups of long grain rice as directed on package. Mound in individual portions with a well in center of each. Place a pat of butter in well, drop in a raw egg yolk and sprinkle with salt and pepper. Mix before eating.

Breaded Chicken Liver Kebobs

12 chicken livers	1 cup chicken broth
Salt, pepper, Ac'cent	2 tablespoons lemon juice
12 slices bacon	
⅔ cup melted butter *or* margarine	1 teaspoon nutmeg
	¼ cup medium sherry
1 cup fine bread crumbs	¼ cup minced parsley

Cut chicken livers into fourths. Sprinkle with salt, pepper and Ac'cent. Cut bacon into 1-inch pieces. Alternate chicken livers and bacon on skewers. Brush with some of the melted butter; roll in crumbs. Grill

4 inches above coals for 10 to 12 minutes or until bacon is crisp, turning often. Meanwhile bring broth to a boil; add remaining melted butter; beat with rotary egg beater until well blended. Add all remaining ingredients except parsley. Slide livers and bacon from skewers onto 4 plates. Pour broth mixture over all. Sprinkle with parsley. *Makes 4 servings. Serve with:* saffron rice and buttered zucchini.

Turkey Kebobs

5 pounds uncooked turkey*, boned
1 cup Rhine wine
⅓ cup soy sauce
½ cup finely chopped onion
1 garlic clove, crushed
1 tablespoon lemon juice
¼ cup vegetable oil
½ teaspoon poultry seasoning

* Buy turkey pieces or quarters. Remove bones and skin.

Cut boned turkey into 1½-inch chunks. Combine remaining ingredients; pour over turkey. Let stand for 1 to 2 hours. Drain, saving marinade. Thread turkey chunks onto skewers; grill 4 inches above hot coals, turning often and brushing with marinade, until browned on all sides and done. Slide off skewers onto plates. *Makes 6 to 8 servings. Serve with:* baked yams, succotash and cranberry sauce. Add a tossed green salad if you wish or a bowl of raw vegetable relishes.

Chicken Shish Kebobs

Chicken meat, cut into 1½-inch chunks
Italian sausage, cut into 1-inch pieces
Medium mushroom caps
Halved chicken livers
Melted butter *or* margarine

String onto skewers, alternating chicken, sausage, mushrooms and chicken livers. Brush with melted butter. Grill 4 inches above heat for 7 minutes. Turn, brush again with melted butter; grill for 7 or 8 minutes longer. (Using fresh rosemary as a brush adds delightful flavor.) *Serve with:* hashed brown potatoes, baby lima beans and a tossed salad.

FISH AND SHELLFISH

Fish Kebobs

**2 pounds firm
    white fish
Marinade***

**2 cucumbers
½ pound bacon
Cherry tomatoes**

Cover fish with marinade; chill for several hours; drain, saving marinade; cut into 1-inch squares. Peel cucumbers; cut into ½-inch slices. Cut bacon into 1-inch pieces. Alternate fish, cucumber slices and bacon on skewers. End with a cherry tomato. Grill 4 inches above coals for about 8 minutes, turning often and basting with marinade. Slide off skewers into toasted frankfurter rolls. *Makes 4 servings. Serve with:* lattice potatoes and avocado and grapefruit salad.

*Marinade

**½ cup vinegar
1 crushed bay leaf
½ teaspoon chervil**

**1 teaspoon salt
Dash Tabasco
⅓ cup vegetable oil**

Combine all ingredients; mix well.

Cape Cod Kebobs

Skewer large clams wrapped in bacon, onion chunks, and halved, canned white potatoes. Brush with melted butter or margarine. Grill 4 inches above coals until bacon is crisp, turning occasionally and brushing with melted butter. To serve, slide off skewers onto plates. *Serve with:* pickled beets, coleslaw and hot rolls.

Fish And Onion Kebobs

3 pounds boned, firm-fleshed fish, such as haddock *or* halibut
12 medium onions, quartered
2 tablespoons lemon *or* lime juice
1 teaspoon sugar
4 bay leaves, crumbled
2 teaspoons rosemary
¼ teaspoon ground cloves
⅓ cup vegetable oil
1 cup claret

Cut fish into 2-inch pieces. Combine with onions. Combine remaining ingredients; mix well; pour over fish and onions. Marinate for at least 1 hour. Alternate fish and onion chunks on skewers. Brush with marinade. Grill 4 inches above coals for about 12 minutes or until fish flakes easily with a fork. Turn twice, brushing with marinade. *Makes 6 servings. Serve with:* French fried potatoes heated in foil on grill, corn on the cob and raw vegetable relishes.

Seaboard Kebobs

2 pounds sea scallops
Melted butter *or* margarine
Salt
Paprika
½ cup wheat germ
1 pound shrimp, cooked, peeled and deveined
1 can (1 lb.) pineapple chunks
4 slices bacon, cut into 1½-inch pieces

Dip scallops into melted butter; sprinkle with salt and paprika; roll in wheat germ. Alternate scallops, shrimp, pineapple chunks and bacon on 6 skewers. Brush shrimp with melted butter. Wrap each skewer in strip of heavy-duty aluminum foil. Grill 4 inches above coals for 10 to 12 minutes, turning once. *Makes 6 servings. Serve with:* shell macaroni salad, raw vegetable relishes and hot cornsticks.

Low Calorie Grilled Fillets Of Sole Apricot

6 sole fillets, each fillet 4 ounces
Salt
1 can (16 oz.) low calorie apricot halves
⅓ cup low calorie Italian salad dressing
Finely chopped chives

Sprinkle fillets with salt and roll up each one like a jelly roll. Cut each fillet roll into halves crosswise. Drain apricots, reserving syrup. Spear fish and apricots alternately onto skewers. Mix reserved fruit syrup and salad dressing. Brush mixture over kebobs. Place on grill 6 inches above hot coals. Cook for 5 minutes on each side, brushing kebobs every 5 minutes with syrup mixture. Sprinkle with chopped chives. Remove from skewers; serve on a platter garnished with parsley and lemon slices. *Makes 6 servings. Serve with:* a salad of raw spinach leaves, cucumbers, sliced radishes, and cooked, chilled green beans.

Salmon Kebobs

2 pounds salmon steak, cut 1½ inches thick
Celery, cut into 1½-inch slices
¾ cup white wine
½ cup vegetable oil
1 tablespoon snipped parsley
1 teaspoon snipped fresh dill
1 teaspoon salt
1 teaspoon paprika

Cut salmon into 1½-inch cubes. Combine with equal number of celery slices. Combine remaining ingredients; mix well; pour over salmon and celery. Let stand for 1 hour. String salmon and celery alternately onto skewers. Grill 4 inches above coals for about 12 minutes. Baste with marinade and turn once during cooking. *Makes 4 servings. Serve with:* instant mashed potatoes, sweet-sour cucumber and onion slices and tomato salad.

California Fish Kebobs

½ to ¾ **pound fresh**
or frozen sea scallops
(about 8 scallops)
1 **pound fresh or**
frozen raw shrimp
(at least 8), shelled
and deveined
¾ **pound halibut steak,**
fresh or frozen, cut
into 1½-inch cubes
(8)

3 **tablespoons**
vegetable oil
¼ **cup lemon juice**
2 **tablespoons capers**
and juice
1 **teaspoon celery seed**
1 **small garlic clove,**
crushed
Dash Tabasco
Gold 'n Crust

Allow frozen fish to thaw in refrigerator. Blend oil, lemon juice, capers, celery seed, garlic and Tabasco in shallow pan. Place shrimp, scallops and fish in oil and lemon juice mixture, turning several times to coat all surfaces well; marinate for about 2 hours in refrigerator. Remove fish from marinade. Lace scallops, shrimp and fish alternately onto four 8- to 10-inch skewers. Sprinkle Gold 'n Crust *evenly* and *generously* on *wet* shrimp, scallops and fish. Place on broiler rack 3 inches from heat source; broil for 5 to 10 minutes, turning once. Or grill 4 inches above coals for 8 to 10 minutes, turning frequently. Don't overcook. Fish is done when it flakes easily when tested with fork. *Makes 4 servings. Serve with:* potato salad and red cabbage slaw.

Skewered Shrimp

Marinate shelled, deveined, raw shrimp in French dressing. Thread shrimp onto skewers, alternating with cherry tomatoes, with lemon slice on end. Broil or grill 3 inches from heat for 3 minutes on each side. Brush with additional French dressing after the first turning. *Serve with:* macaroni salad and raw vegetable relishes.

Sea Scallop Kebobs

1 medium onion,
   finely grated
3 tablespoons lime
   juice
½ teaspoon salt
1 teaspoon sugar

¼ teaspoon coarse
   black pepper
2 pounds sea scallops
Melted butter *or*
   margarine

Combine onion, lime juice, salt, sugar and pepper; pour over scallops; stir until scallops are coated. Cover; chill for 2 hours, turning scallops several times. Thread scallops close together onto skewers. Brush generously with melted butter. Broil or grill 4 inches from heat for about 10 minutes, turning often and basting with melted butter. Slide off skewers to serve. Garnish with lime wedges. *Makes 4 to 6 servings. Serve with:* French fried potatoes, buttered zucchini and a tomato and cucumber salad.

Variation:
Thread squares of partially cooked bacon between scallops.

Shrimp And Bacon Kebobs

2 pounds shrimp,
   fresh *or* frozen *or*
1½ pounds peeled and
   deveined shrimp
1 cup flour
1 tablespoon
   paprika
1 teaspoon salt

1 can *or* bottle
   (12 oz.) beer
Lemon juice
Oil for frying
4 slices bacon,
   partially cooked
Pineapple chunks
Whole canned
   mushrooms

Clean shrimp if necessary. If shrimp are frozen, let thaw on paper toweling to absorb moisture. Combine flour, paprika and salt; gradually beat in beer until batter is quite thin. Squeeze a little lemon juice over shrimp; dip the shrimp into additional flour, then into the batter. Deep fry at 400° for 3 to 5 minutes or until batter is golden brown. Drain on paper towels. Cut each slice of partially cooked bacon into four pieces. On skewers alternate cooked shrimp with bacon, pineapple and mushrooms. Before serving, place kebobs under broiler just to crisp bacon and heat shrimp through. Serve on a bed of rice with sweet-sour sauce or creole sauce. *Makes 4 servings. Serve with:* stuffed baked potatoes, broccoli and a salad of sliced beets and onion rings.

East Indian Curried Shrimp Kebobs

1½ **pounds shrimp,**
fresh or frozen or
1 **pound peeled and**
deveined shrimp
1 **cup pineapple chunks**

1 **green pepper, cut into**
1-inch squares
4 **preserved kumquats**
Curry Basting Sauce*

Clean shrimp if necessary. If shrimp are frozen, let thaw on paper toweling to absorb moisture. Thread shrimp, pineapple chunks, pepper squares and kumquats alternately onto skewers. Brush with Curry Basting Sauce. Place in preheated broiler 3 inches from heat and broil for 5 minutes on each side, until shrimp turn pink. Brush with additional basting sauce after first turning. *Makes 4 to 6 servings. Serve with:* rice, green peas and raw vegetable relishes.

*Curry Basting Sauce

1 **garlic clove, crushed**
2 **tablespoons butter**
or margarine

1¼ **teaspoons curry**
powder
¾ **teaspoon salt**
1¼ **cups water**

Sauté garlic in butter or margarine. Add curry powder; cook for about 2 minutes. Add salt and water. Cook, uncovered, for about 10 minutes.

Kebobs Neptune

1 pound shrimp
Lemon Butter Sauce*
1 pound sea scallops

12 large pimiento-
stuffed olives

Cook, shell and devein shrimp. Marinate for about 1
hour in Lemon Butter Sauce. Drain, saving sauce. Alternate shrimp, scallops and olives on skewers. Grill 3
inches from heat for about 3 minutes on each side,
brushing with sauce and turning often. Do not overcook. *Makes 6 kebobs. Serve with:* lattice potatoes and
grapefruit and avocado salad.

*Lemon Butter Sauce

¼ cup butter *or*
margarine

¼ cup lemon juice

Melt butter; stir in lemon juice; keep warm.

Shrimp Fruit Kebobs

1 cup orange juice
½ cup vinegar
½ cup vegetable oil
½ cup soy sauce
1 teaspoon salt
1 pound fresh shrimp,
shelled and
deveined, *or*

1 package (10 *or*
12 oz.) frozen
shrimp, thawed
16 thin slices lime *or*
lemon
16 maraschino cherries
1 large banana,
cut into thick slices

Combine orange juice, vinegar, oil, soy sauce, and
salt; blend. Add remaining ingredients. Chill for 1
hour. Arrange shrimp, lime or lemon slices, cherries,
and banana slices on 8 skewers. Reserve marinade.
Broil kebobs 3 to 4 inches from source of heat, or cook
on outdoor grill 4 inches above coals for 3 to 4 minutes on each side. Heat remaining marinade and serve
as a sauce with kebobs. *Makes 4 servings. Serve with:*
potato chips, carrot sticks, and celery stuffed with
cream cheese.

Shrimp Kebobs With Herb Marinade

2 pounds large shrimp, uncooked
1 cup vegetable oil
1 teaspoon salt
1 tablespoon dried parsley
1 tablespoon dried basil leaves
2 garlic cloves, minced
1 tablespoon catchup
¼ teaspoon Tabasco
2 tablespoons tarragon vinegar
1 teaspoon sugar

Shell and devein shrimp. Place in shallow dish. Combine remaining ingredients; pour over shrimp; cover. Chill for 3 hours. Drain shrimp, saving marinade. Thread shrimp onto skewers. Grill 3 inches above coals for 3 minutes, basting with marinade. Turn; grill for 5 minutes longer, basting several times. *Makes 4 to 6 servings. Serve with:* potato salad, green pepper cole-slaw and relishes.

VEAL

Veal and Bacon Kebobs

3 pounds boneless
    veal
Salt
Pepper
Ac'cent

2 garlic cloves,
    minced
½ cup vegetable oil
½ pound bacon
Melted butter or
    margarine

Cut veal into 1-inch cubes. Sprinkle with salt, pepper and Ac'cent. Add garlic and ½ cup oil; stir to coat veal. Refrigerate for 2 hours. Cut bacon into 1-inch squares. Drain veal; thread veal and bacon alternately on skewers. Grill 4 inches above heat for about 20 minutes, or until veal is done and bacon crisp. Before serving, brush with melted butter or margarine. *Makes 6 servings. Serve with:* minted new potatoes, green peas and a cucumber and scallion salad.

Harvest Kebobs

½ cup honey
 1 can frozen orange
    juice concentrate
⅓ cup finely diced
    crystallized ginger
 1 teaspoon lemon
    juice

½ teaspoon oregano
 2 pounds boneless
    veal
 1 acorn squash
    (unpared)
 4 medium apples
    (unpared)

Combine first 5 ingredients; mix thoroughly. Cut veal into 1-inch cubes. Cut squash into 2-inch pieces; cook for 10 minutes. Cut cored apples into quarters. Pour orange mixture over veal. Cover; refrigerate for several hours, turning veal cubes occasionally; drain, saving marinade. Thread veal, squash and apples alternately onto 4 long skewers. Grill 3 inches above coals for about 30 minutes, turning often and brushing with reserved marinade. Slide food off skewers onto plates. *Makes 4 servings. Serve with:* potatoes baked in foil on the grill and a tossed salad.

Maui Kebobs

Cut 1½ pounds veal into 1½-inch cubes. Marinate for 2 hours in Sauce*. Drain meat, saving marinade. Thread meat onto skewers. Broil about 4 inches above coals for 20 to 25 minutes, turning often and basting with marinade. *Makes 4 servings. Serve with:* rice, green beans with mushrooms and pineapple salad.

*Sauce

3 **tablespoons instant minced onion**	½ **teaspoon ground ginger**
1 **teaspoon chili powder**	1 **teaspoon salt**
1 **teaspoon tumeric**	¼ **cup lemon juice**
	1 **tablespoon honey**

Combine all ingredients; mix well.

SAUSAGES AND COLD CUTS

Frankfurter Kebobs

1 cup chili sauce	3 drops Tabasco
1 to 2 tablespoons brown sugar	3 slices onion
	12 frankfurters
3 tablespoons vinegar	8 slices bacon

Combine chili sauce, brown sugar, vinegar, Tabasco and onion in saucepan. Simmer for 5 minutes. Cut each frankfurter into quarters and each slice of bacon into 6 pieces. Arrange alternately on skewers. Place on baking sheet and spread with half the sauce. Broil for 5 minutes under moderate heat. Turn; spread with remaining sauce. Broil for 5 minutes longer. *Makes 6 servings. Serve with:* baked beans, hot, crusty rolls and apple coleslaw.

Frankfurter-Bacon Kebobs

3 slices bacon	Sweet-Sour Sauce*
6 frankfurters	

Cut each bacon slice into 6 pieces. Cut frankfurters crosswise into fourths. Thread 4 skewers with alternate pieces of bacon and frankfurters. Grill 4 inches above coals until light brown, turning often. Brush with Sweet-Sour sauce; turn; grill for 5 minutes; turn; brush again with sauce; grill for 5 minutes longer. Slide off skewers into frankfurter rolls. *Makes 4 servings. Serve with:* any remaining sauce, corn chips, salad of garden vegetables.

*Sweet-Sour Sauce

1 cup chili sauce
3 tablespoons vinegar
Few drops Tabasco

1 tablespoon brown sugar
1 small onion, sliced

Combine all ingredients; simmer for 5 minutes.

All-Hot Kebobs

6 frankfurters
1 tablespoon vegetable oil
1 can (10½ oz.) pizza sauce

12 pieces green pepper, about 1 inch each
12 canned pineapple chunks

Cut frankfurters into thirds. Place frankfurters in a bowl. Combine oil and pizza sauce; pour over frankfurters. Marinate in refrigerator for at least two hours. Using 3 frankfurter pieces, 2 green pepper pieces and 2 pineapple chunks per skewer, alternate the food on 6 skewers, starting and ending with piece of frankfurter. Place skewers in shallow pie plate or on a rack, about 4 inches from heat. Broil for about 4 minutes on one side, basting with marinade during broiling. Turn and broil on second side for 4 minutes longer, basting several times. Slide off skewers into toasted frankfurter rolls. *Makes 6 kebobs. Serve with:* home-fried potatoes and a salad of cooked mixed vegetables.

Hot Dogs On A Stick

Cut frankfurters into fourths, crosswise. Thread end of bacon slice onto skewer, then alternate frankfurter pieces and pineapple chunks onto skewer, weaving bacon strip over and under, skewering at the other end. Grill 4 inches above coals for about 15 minutes, turning often. Slide off into hot frankfurter rolls. *Serve with:* potato chips, green pepper coleslaw and carrot sticks.

Weiner Special

1 **pound frankfurters,**
 cut into 1-inch
 slices
1 **cup celery, cut into**
 1-inch slices
1 **cup onions, cut into**
 1-inch slices

1 **cup green pepper,**
 cut into 1-inch
 squares
6 **large pitted black**
 olives
Soy and Herb
 Marinade*

Combine frankfurter pieces and vegetables. Cover with marinade. Let stand for about 3 hours; drain, saving marinade. Alternate frankfurter pieces and vegetables on 6 skewers, ending with a black olive. Broil 4 inches above glowing coals for 5 minutes on each side, brushing often with marinade. Slide off skewers into toasted frankfurter rolls. *Makes 6 servings. Serve with:* hot buttered French bread and a tomato salad.

***Soy and Herb Marinade**

½ **cup soy sauce**
⅓ **cup catchup**
¼ **cup vegetable oil**
¼ **cup wine vinegar**

½ **teaspoon thyme**
½ **teaspoon savory**
¼ **cup minced chives**
1 **teaspoon prepared**
 mustard

Combine all ingredients; mix well.

Campfire Kebobs

8 **frankfurters**
1 **pound sharp**
 cheddar cheese,
 unsliced

8 **slices bacon, halved**
16 **sweet gherkins**
16 **cherry tomatoes**

Cut each frankfurter into 3 pieces. Cut cheese into 1½-inch pieces and wrap each piece in bacon. String onto 8 skewers, alternating 3 frankfurter pieces, 2 gherkins, 2 tomatoes and 2 cheese and bacon chunks on each, ending with frankfurter. Grill 4 inches above coals until bacon is crisp, turning often. *Makes 4 servings. Serve with:* potato salad, green pepper coleslaw, celery and carrot sticks.

Frank Kebobs With Kraut

2 **medium green peppers**	3½ **cups undrained sauerkraut**
1 **pound frankfurters, cut into 1½-inch pieces**	4 **tablespoons butter *or* margarine, divided**
1 **medium cucumber, sliced**	½ **teaspoon salt**
¾ **pound small white onions, peeled and parboiled (5 minutes)***	⅛ **teaspoon pepper**
	4 **tablespoons brown sugar, divided**
	½ **cup chopped onion**

* 1 can (1 lb.) boiled onions may be substituted for the parboiled onions.

Cut 1½ green peppers into 1-inch squares; chop remaining ½ pepper. Alternate frankfurter pieces, cucumber slices, parboiled onions and green pepper pieces on skewers to make 8 kebobs. Drain sauerkraut, reserving ½ cup liquid. Combine kraut liquid, 2 tablespoons butter, salt, pepper and 2 tablespoons brown sugar in small saucepan. Heat just until butter is melted. Brush kraut-liquid mixture over kebobs and let stand for about 1 hour before cooking. Broil kebobs for 7 minutes on each side, or until done. Meanwhile, prepare a bed of kraut for kebobs by sautéing kraut in remaining 2 tablespoons butter with chopped onion and chopped green pepper. Stir in remaining 2 tablespoons brown sugar. Serve kraut warm with kebobs. *Makes 8 servings. Serve with:* hot potato salad, scallions and radishes.

Bologna-Cheese Kebobs

1 pound unsliced
bologna
½ pound unsliced,
sharp cheddar
cheese

Dill pickles
Chili Barbecue Sauce*

Cut bologna, cheese and pickles into 1-inch chunks. Alternate on oiled skewers. Brush with Chili Barbecue Sauce. Grill 4 inches above hot coals for about 15 minutes, turning often and basting with sauce.

*Chili Barbecue Sauce

1 cup chili sauce
2 teaspoons vinegar
½ teaspoon sugar
2 teaspoons prepared
mustard

½ teaspoon Worcester-
shire sauce
2 tablespoons bottled
Italian dressing

Combine all ingredients; mix well; heat to boiling. Simmer for 5 minutes. *Makes about 1¼ cups.*

Hobo Kebobs

Buy unsliced bologna sausage. Cut into 1½-inch chunks. On skewers alternate bologna chunks, thick onion slices and dill pickle chunks. Brush with bottled Italian dressing. Grill 4 to 5 inches above hot coals for 15 minutes. Turn, brush again with Italian dressing, grill for 15 minutes longer. Slip off skewers into toasted frankfurter rolls. *Serve with:* kidney beans and carrot coleslaw.

Kebobs And Beans

Skewer pickled onions, small squares of green pepper, folded bologna slices and cherry tomatoes ending with bologna. Do not cook. *Serve with:* baked beans and Boston brown bread.

Kebobs With Spaghetti

1 can (12 oz.) luncheon meat
1 can (1 lb.) pineapple chunks
2 tablespoons butter *or* margarine

2 cans (15¼ oz. each) spaghetti in tomato sauce
¼ teaspoon Tabasco

Cut luncheon meat crosswise into 4 slices. Cut slices in half lengthwise, then crosswise into fourths to make 32 cubes. Arrange meat cubes and pineapple chunks alternately on 6 8-inch skewers. Melt butter in skillet. Add kebobs; brown over medium heat, turning occasionally. Remove from skillet; keep warm. Add spaghetti; stir in Tabasco. Heat to serving temperature and arrange kebobs over top. *Makes 6 servings. Serve with:* hot garlic bread and a green salad.

Brunch Kebobs

String halved brown and serve sausages, canned apricot or small peach halves and canned broiled mushroom crowns on skewers. Brush with melted butter or margarine. Grill 3 inches above coals for about 5 minutes; turn; brush again with melted butter; grill for 5 minutes longer. *Serve with:* hot rolls, carrot curls, celery stuffed with blue cheese.

Sausage And Pineapple Kebobs

Cut brown and serve pork sausages in half, crosswise. Cut bacon into 1-inch pieces. Drain tiny canned white potatoes, and pineapple chunks. String sausage halves, bacon, potatoes and pineapple chunks onto skewers. Brush with melted butter or margarine and grill 3 inches above coals until golden brown on all sides. *Serve with:* hot, crusty rolls and Waldorf salad.

Elegant Brunch Waffles
With Sausage Kebobs

Creamed Eggs

1 cup sliced fresh
  mushrooms
6 tablespoons butter
  or margarine,
  divided
¼ cup all-purpose
  flour

1 teaspoon salt
¼ teaspoon pepper
¼ teaspoon dry mustard
2 cups milk
6 hard-cooked eggs,
  sliced

Sauté mushrooms in 2 tablespoons butter in small skillet. Melt remaining butter in medium-sized saucepan. Stir in flour, salt, pepper and dry mustard. Cook 1 minute over low heat, stirring constantly. Gradually add milk; blend well. Cook over medium heat, stirring constantly until thickened. Stir in mushrooms and eggs; heat thoroughly.

Kebobs

12 brown and serve
   sausage links,
   thawed
12 cherry tomatoes

1 package (9 oz.)
  frozen waffles
Parsley

Cut sausage links in half. Alternate sausage pieces and tomatoes on 7- or 8-inch metal skewers. Broil about 6 inches from source of heat for about 3 minutes. Turn; broil an additional 3 minutes or until sausage is browned. Meanwhile, prepare waffles in toaster or oven according to package directions. For each serving, top 2 waffle sections with creamed eggs; garnish with parsley. *Makes 6 servings. Serve with:* broiled kebobs.

COMBINATIONS OF MEATS

Use your favorite marinade, barbecue sauce *or* melted butter *or* margarine for brushing and basting. Grill as usual.

1. One-inch slices of knockwurst, cherry tomatoes, onion chunks.
2. Chunks of knockwurst *or* frankfurters wrapped in a bacon spiral.
3. Small fish balls, bacon squares, crisp pickle slices.
4. Chunks of rock lobster tails, mushroom crowns, bacon squares, pitted black olives.
5. Oysters, bacon squares, shrimp and cocktail onions.
6. Cheese sandwiches cut into 1½-inch squares, dill pickle slices, pineapple chunks and 1-inch beef cubes.
7. Vienna sausages, apple wedges, cubes of French bread drenched in melted butter *or* margarine.
8. Chunks of cooked chicken or turkey, 1-inch slices of celery, watermelon pickles, cherry tomatoes.

Kebob Medley

2 pounds lean, tender beef, cut into 2-inch squares
1 pound boned lamb, cut into 2-inch squares
Marinade*
Salt
6 firm medium tomatoes, peeled and quartered, *or* 12 cherry tomatoes
6 medium onions, peeled and quartered
6 medium green peppers, seeded and cut into fourths

Trim fat from meat. Mark lamb with wooden picks. Place meat in large bowl; pour marinade over meat. Marinate for at least 2 hours; drain; save marinade. Skewer meat and vegetables, threading vegetables (except tomatoes) between pieces of meat. Use 2 cubes of beef to 1 of lamb. Remove picks from lamb. Line broiler pan with foil. Preheat broiler. Brush skewered food with oil, then liberally with marinade. Broil 4 inches below heat for 10 minutes. Turn. Place tomatoes on tips of skewers. Brush with marinade. Broil for 3 to 5 minutes longer, or until meat reaches desired doneness. Wreath a large platter with parsley. Slip meat and vegetables off skewers, making a ring inside parsley. Fill center with hot fluffy rice. *Makes 8 servings. Serve* : at once with a tossed salad.

*Marinade

Juice of ½ large lemon (1½ tablespoons)
1½ cups red wine
2 teaspoons grated orange peel
½ cup orange juice
½ cup vegetable oil
2 tablespoons soy sauce
1 garlic clove, pressed
2 slices onion
2 teaspoons nutmeg
2 teaspoons curry powder
2 teaspoons ginger
2 teaspoons chili powder

Combine marinade ingredients; mix well.

Mixed Grill Kebobs

4 lamb kidneys   6 loin lamb chops
1 calf's heart   ½ pound bacon
½ pound calf's liver   Bottled Italian dressing

Remove membranes and fat from kidneys and heart.
Cut into 1-inch pieces. Cut liver into 1-inch pieces. Cut
lean section of each chop into 3 pieces (use bones and
remaining meat for making soup or stew). Cut bacon
into 1-inch pieces. Cover meats, except bacon, with
dressing. Chill for at least 3 hours. Drain, saving dressing. Thread meats alternately onto skewers. Brush with
dressing. Grill 4 inches above coals until bacon is crisp
and meats are done (about 15 minutes), turning often
and brushing with dressing. *Makes 6 servings. Serve
with:* au gratin potatoes, raw spinach and tomato salad.

Shish Kebobs

2½ pounds veal—cut   2 cups Chablis
    into 1½-inch   4 green peppers
    squares, 1 inch   1 cup Chelois
    thick (40 pieces)   40 strips bacon
2½ pounds lamb—cut   40 medium mushroom
    into 1½-inch   caps
    squares, 1 inch   20 cherry tomatoes
    thick (40 pieces)

Marinate meat squares in Chablis for several hours.
Cut each green pepper into ten equal strips. Marinate
vegetables in Chelois for several hours. Simmer meat
for 5 to 8 minutes in Chablis. Slice each strip of bacon
in half and wrap around a cube of meat. Arrange on 20
skewers in this order: mushroom cap, veal, pepper,
lamb, tomato, veal, pepper, lamb and mushroom cap.
Broil, with surface of food 3 inches below heat for 12
to 15 minutes, turning often. Or grill 3 to 4 inches
above coals for 15 to 20 minutes. *Makes 20 portions. Serve with:* herbed rice, green peas with
onions and a tossed salad.

Ham And Beef Kebobs

1½ to 2 pounds lean,
   tender beef
½ pound ready-to-eat
   ham, unsliced
8 medium
   mushrooms

8 small canned onions
Melted butter *or*
   margarine
8 cherry tomatoes

Cut beef into 16 cubes and ham into 8 cubes. String 8 skewers, using 2 cubes of beef, 1 cube of ham, 1 mushroom and 1 onion on each. Brush with melted butter. Grill over hot coals until beef reaches desired degree of doneness. Slip a cherry tomato onto end of each skewer. Grill a minute or two longer. Slip off skewers onto plates or into hot frankfurter rolls. *Makes 6 servings. Serve with:* canned kidney beans and apple coleslaw.

Lamb And Salami Kebobs

6 lamb steaks, 1 inch
   thick
1 pound salami,
   unsliced
2 large onions, sliced
2 garlic cloves,
   crushed

⅓ cup vegetable oil
3 tablespoons soy sauce
3 tablespoons vinegar
2 teaspoons sugar
Dash Tabasco

Cut lamb and salami into 1-inch cubes. Place in shallow pan. Arrange onions on top. Combine remaining ingredients; pour into pan. Cover. Refrigerate for several hours or overnight. Remove onions. Drain meat, saving sauce; string onto skewers. Broil over hot coals for about 15 minutes, turning often. Cook onions in remaining sauce until golden brown. Serve with kebobs. *Makes 6 to 8 servings. Serve with:* macaroni and cheese, Italian green beans and a tossed salad.

Lamb And Chicken Livers En Brochette

2 pounds lean lamb
Marinade*
12 bacon slices, halved

8 chicken livers, cut into 24 pieces
16 medium mushroom caps

Cut lamb into 24 cubes. Pour marinade over lamb; refrigerate for about 3 hours. Wrap a half-strip of bacon around each piece of chicken liver. Drain lamb, saving marinade. Alternate 3 lamb cubes, 3 wrapped chicken livers, and 2 mushrooms on each of 8 skewers. Brush with marinade. Grill 4 inches above heat for about 15 minutes, turning often and basting with marinade. *Makes 4 servings. Serve with:* poppy seed noodles, asparagus and a tomato salad.

*Marinade

½ cup vegetable oil
1 cup dry red wine
1 medium onion, minced

1 garlic clove, minced
1 teaspoon tarragon
1 teaspoon salt
¼ teaspoon Tabasco

Combine all ingredients; mix well.

Far Eastern Kebobs

¾ cup soy sauce
⅓ cup sugar
¼ cup vegetable oil
¼ cup dry sherry
1 teaspoon Ac'cent

1 garlic clove, minced
1 pound veal
1 pound lean beef
1 pound pork tenderloin

Combine first 6 ingredients; mix well. Cut meats into 1½-inch cubes. Pour soy mixture over meats. Chill for 3 hours, turning meat cubes occasionally. Drain, saving marinade. Alternate meats on skewers, spacing cubes ¼ inch apart. Grill 4 inches above coals for 30 minutes, turning often and basting with marinade. *Makes 6 servings. Serve with:* vegetable kebobs (page 00) and rice.

VARIETY MEATS

Calf's Liver Kebobs

1½ pounds calf's liver, sliced 1 inch thick	½ teaspoon powdered cinnamon
1 garlic clove, crushed	¼ teaspoon powdered cloves
½ cup yogurt	1 tablespoon ground coriander
¼ teaspoon Tabasco	Melted bacon drippings *or* butter
1 teaspoon powdered ginger	

Cut liver into 1-inch cubes. Combine all remaining ingredients except drippings; pour over liver. Marinate for several hours. Drain liver; thread onto skewers. Brush with melted drippings. (If desired, partially cooked squares of bacon may be inserted between cubes of liver). Grill 4 inches above coals to desired degree of doneness, turning often and brushing with drippings. *Makes 4 to 6 servings. Serve with:* canned fried onion rings heated in foil on grill, hashed brown potatoes and tomato salad.

Lamb Kidneys And Bacon En Brochette

Use 2 lamb kidneys, 1 slice bacon and 3 mushroom caps per skewer. Wash kidneys in cold water. Remove outer membrane; split; remove white veins and fat.

Simmer until tender in water to which a little lemon or lime juice has been added. Cool slightly; cut into quarters. Thread bacon slice onto skewer, then a piece of kidney, then a mushroom, then the bacon strip. Repeat, with bacon running like a ribbon on the skewer. Repeat until all ingredients are used. Grill 3 inches above coals for about 7 minutes. Turn; broil for 5 to 7 minutes longer. Sprinkle with salt and pepper. *Makes 4 servings. Serve with:* canned fried onion rings heated in foil on grill, grilled tomatoes and canned macaroni and cheese heated in saucepan on the grill.

Sweetbreads En Brochette

1 **pound veal sweet-**
   breads
2 **teaspoons salt,**
   divided
6 **tablespoons lemon**
   juice, divided
24 **small mushrooms**
2 **teaspoons Wor-**
   cestershire sauce

¼ **teaspoon Tabasco**
12 **bacon slices, halved**
   crosswise
Melted butter *or*
   margarine
Snipped parsley

Simmer sweetbreads 20 minutes in water to cover. Add 1 teaspoon salt and 1 tablespoon lemon juice for each quart of water. Drain; cool slightly; hold under cold running water; slip off membrane. Cut out dark veins and thick connective tissue. Cut sweetbreads into 24 chunks. Remove stems from mushrooms; place crowns in bowl. Combine remaining lemon juice, Worcestershire sauce, Tabasco, remaining salt; pour over mushrooms. Chill, stirring occasionally. Roll up halves of bacon strips. On each of six skewers, alternate sweetbread chunks, mushroom crowns and bacon rolls. Arrange in shallow, open pan. Brush with melted butter. Broil 6 inches below heat, turning often and brushing with butter, for 15 to 20 minutes or until golden brown. Pour on remaining butter; sprinkle with parsley. *Makes 4 servings. Serve with:* lattice potatoes, green peas with onions and a salad of sliced tomatoes and onion rings.

Swiss Liver And Bacon Kebobs

1½ **pounds calf's liver;**
    sliced ¾ inch thick
 20 **dried sage leaves**
 10 **bacon slices,**
    halved crosswise
 ½ **cup butter or**
    margarine,
    divided
 ¼ **cup vegetable oil**

2 **tablespoons**
  minced onion
2 **pkgs. (10 oz. each)**
  frozen chopped
  spinach, thawed
¼ **teaspoon garlic**
  powder
½ **teaspoon salt**
Pepper
¼ **cup dry white wine**

Cut liver into 1-inch squares. Wrap each piece of liver and 1 sage leaf in each piece of bacon. Thread 5 wrapped pieces of liver onto each of 4 6-inch skewers, pressing them together. Melt 3 tablespoons butter in large, heavy skillet; add oil. When very hot, arrange skewers in skillet. Cook over moderate heat, turning occasionally, until bacon is crisp (about 12 minutes). Meanwhile melt remaining butter in another large skillet. Add onion; cook until soft but not brown. Drain spinach; squeeze dry; spread in skillet. Add garlic powder, salt and pepper. Cook and stir until spinach is heated through. Spread spinach on heated platter; arrange skewers on top. Pour off fat in which skewers were cooked; pour in wine; bring to boil, stirring constantly, and scraping up any brown particles on bottom of pan. Pour over skewered liver. *Makes 4 servings. Serve with:* mashed potatoes and sliced tomatoes and cucumbers in French dressing.

Lamb Kidney Kebobs

12 **lamb kidneys**
 6 **slices bacon, halved**
   crosswise
 ½ **cup red wine**

2 **tablespoons**
  vegetable oil
½ **teaspoon dried mint**
12 **cherry tomatoes**

Split kidneys in half lengthwise, cut away fat and tubes. Fold bacon pieces. Combine wine, oil and mint. Thread kidneys, folded bacon pieces and tomatoes onto skewers. Be sure kidneys are skewered so that they will lie flat. Brush with oil mixture. Broil 4 inches below heat for about 10 minutes, turning often and brushing with oil mixture. *Makes 6 servings. Serve with:* creamed potatoes, broccoli, hot baking powder biscuits and a tossed salad.

Liver And Bacon En Brochette

2 **pounds calf's liver, cut 1½ inches thick**	2 **tablespoons vegetable oil**
12 **medium mushroom caps**	1 **tablespoon wine vinegar**
12 **slices bacon**	1 **teaspoon sugar**
	¼ **teaspoon basil**

Thread liver, mushrooms and bacon onto skewers. Twine bacon strips over and under food on skewers. Combine oil, vinegar, sugar and basil; brush over kebobs. Broil 4 inches below heat until bacon is crisp, turning often and brushing with oil mixture (about 10 minutes). *Makes 6 servings. Serve with:* scalloped potatoes, green peas and raw relishes.

Index